Strategic CaseMaking™

The Field Guide for Building Public and Political Will

Tiffany Manuel, PhD

The CaseMade Press

Orlando, Florida

Strategic CaseMaking™: The Field Guide for Building Public and Political Will

Published in the United States by TheCaseMade Press, an imprint of Dr. Tiffany Manuel, LLC.

Larger quantities of this book may be purchased for educational, business or sales promotions by emailing: Admin@TheCaseMade.com.

This Field Guide is updated frequently with additional modules, learning guides, examples and case studies. For more information or to get regular updates, please visit: www.TheCaseMade.com. This is the second edition.

Library of Congress Cataloging-in-Publication Data has been applied for.

ISBN 978-1-7348685-0-0

For My Mom, Charline Manuel,
an accomplished author in her own right,
who inspires me every day to be better.

For my sons,
Madu and Caleb,
to whom I hope to leave a better world.

"A genuine leader is not a searcher of consensus, but a molder of consensus.

Reverend, Dr. Martin Luther King, Jr.

Strategic CaseMaking™

Perhaps more than at any point in our history, we need to utilize and model more effective ways of building public will. Improving the way that we make the case for change, is one of the most powerful ways to build the public will we need to tackle the tough issues that threaten, constrain and shape, our communities. Building stronger public support may seem daunting and complicated but it doesn't have to be so hard.

At **TheCaseMade**, we work with hundreds of passionate social change leaders, changemakers and innovators around the United States who are building better, stronger communities that are diverse, equitable and inclusive. By aligning their community stakeholders around the kind of deep systems changes that can improve outcomes for all people, these leaders are able to grow their impact, scale their programs, and catalyze the investments they need to improve their communities. This Field Guide articulates the core ideas, concepts and principles of our approach, Strategic CaseMaking™ and is divided into several broad sections.

What's Inside This Field Guide?
- Understanding What It Means to Build Public Will in the Current Political and Economic Environment
- Review of the Strategic CaseMaking™ Approach, along with a Series of Thoughtful Reflection Questions, Guides, Examples & Resources for Deploying the Principles in Your Materials
- Practice Pages to Get You Started Immediately

Table of Contents

The single biggest failure of leadership is to treat adaptive challenges and system problems like they are simple technical problems.

Getting Serious About Solving the Challenges Affecting Our Communities

Most of the toughest problems we face today are adaptive, rather than technical. A technical problem is one that can be fixed with a single or momentary solution. Often, a single discovery or technological development is required to fix our technical problems. Losing Wi-Fi is a technical problem. You can just restart the router and the hair-pulling chaos that ensued from being temporarily disconnected and inconvenienced, is immediately relieved and quickly forgotten.

An adaptive challenge takes broader alignment of a wide range of stakeholders (usually with differing perspectives, objectives and goals) to solve. Adaptive challenges usually require significant redesign of the systems that govern our lives – the educational system, the workforce development system, the housing delivery system, the health care and delivery system, the transportation system, the criminal justice system and many more. Rarely do we think about how many different systems are at work behind the scenes, determining many of the outcomes in our lives. Getting alignment across the agencies that manage these systems as well as the broader set of stakeholder groups when those systems need to be redesigned takes time and deliberate thoughtful action.

Adaptive challenges also take time because they usually require shifts in culture, practice, mindset, processes and relationships between many people and institutions. Solving homelessness in our country, or the opioid epidemic; providing health insurance to all Americans or addressing the racial wealth gap — are all examples of adaptive challenges that require adaptive approaches. They require political will. They require public will. They require people in all walks of life getting involved and being willing to change their attitudes, their preconceptions, their fears, their approaches, and their strategies. Most adaptive challenges require that we deliberate, collectively problem-solve, and take action together.

When we treat adaptive challenges like technical problems, it renders our communities unable to implement even the most basic system reforms. For example, we know how to build affordable homes and with the use of technology, we are learning how to build them faster and more cost efficiently. Yet the challenges of affordable housing persist because we have not solved the adaptive challenges around housing.

For example, how will we allocate the resources to build and maintain housing for families with low incomes? How will we overcome not-in-my-backyard attitudes that would enable us to build housing where there is land? How do we overcome public beliefs that affordable housing is a commodity and a consumer good rather than a public good that we all benefit from? How do we get ordinary Americans to see the value of providing housing or health care or quality education to many of the most economically vulnerable communities?

Our inability to recognize these issues as adaptive challenges means that, these challenges persist, on many other issues, even though we have the technical means to solve them. There are no silver bullets for adaptive challenges — especially those that require system change to solve. They can only be solved by redesigning how government, corporations, nonprofits, houses of worship, community-based organizations and many others, change how they do their work. Overcoming adaptive challenges requires authentic community engagement, continuous support, time to adapt (hence, "adaptive" leadership) and a public will-building strategy that can provide ongoing support for this work.

The Strategic CaseMaking™ discussed in this field guide is an adaptive approach to building the support we need to tackle tough issues. It was specifically designed to address these types of challenges. Here we define the ideal "problem" for Strategic CaseMaking™ as a challenge or problem facing a community that cannot be solved by one decision-maker, organization, agency, corporation, community group or investment.

Your case (or argument for a particular solution) is likely to be an adaptive challenge if it requires shifts in regulations, policies, investments, or other actions at a level of scale that can only be achieved by aligning a multitude of stakeholders, across sectors, neighborhoods, communities, organizations and groups.

It is perhaps most important to say that adaptive challenges require **inclusive** system change, almost by definition. That is, you cannot solve adaptive challenges without aligning a wide range of stakeholders and strategic partners.

Many worthy, well-defined issues that need a stronger case to build public will for creating fair and just opportunities for all people to reach their potential for health and well-being, could benefit from this approach.

What Adaptive Leadership Looks Like?

 Systems Orientation That Focuses on Root Cause

 Requires Support & Alignment Across a Wide Range of Stakeholders

 People and Outcomes Focused

 Requires People to Shift Mindset, Perspective, Understanding & Knowledge

 Solutions Encourage Innovation, Spread, and Scale

 Public Deliberation & Collective Problem Solving

 Requires Capacity Building Around New Strategies

 Data-Informed, Evidence-Based Strategies, Clear Success Metrics Tracked Over Time

Adaptive, collaborative leaders understand the importance of public will building and the intentionally courageous work that it requires.

The Urgency to Build Public Will

We are fortunate to live in a time of enormous opportunity and potential. The technological advances that we've made over the last century, have made our lives possible beyond measure. By many metrics and indicators, we have made significant progress in advancing the economic, social and health of our communities.

While we may have made these important advances and our future is bright, there remains much to be done. We do not want to take the old challenges of inequality, poverty, and social exclusion into our future. We do not want to continue to kill our environment or our planet.

Yet, many of the systems that govern our communities have not been truly updated for decades, so they continue to exacerbate old inequalities – creating more inequalities, problems to solve, and distance between the "haves" and the "have nots". Whole regions across the United States are today splintering into separate, antagonistic and vastly unequal political, social and economic groups. Old dividing lines of race, gender, and class are today joined by new divisions along the lines of religion, political party, sexual orientation and more. Perhaps most important, our ability to have civil discourse about these issues and to problem-solve together, is deeply broken.

In this context, social changemakers who are trying to improve the communities in which they live face stiff headwinds. Those headwinds get even stronger when those changemakers are trying to make a strong case for the outcomes that are hardest to achieve: equitable and inclusive system change. While we are often working to build political will, it is broad public support (or outrage) that enables the kind of scale needed to transform systems and enact longer-term, more impactful solutions.

The work to build the public will may be tougher than many of us realize. While we are lifting data, policy and programmatic solutions, we are often missing the opportunity to change the narrative about *why our solutions matter* for everybody, even when they are targeted to people who are most in need; *why we have a collective responsibility* for solving these issues and *what system changes are needed* to advance better outcomes for all.

Moreover, the way in which we (as community advocates, organizers, investors, and changemakers) are engaging policymakers and everyday Americans ostensibly to take action on these problems, has been largely counter-productive. I am often astounded by well-intentioned "public awareness" campaigns that reinforce implicit bias around race, class and gender. Or lobbying campaigns that seek short-term wins by inadvertently reinforcing the worst stereotypes, narratives and ingrained beliefs of our citizens.

And I am especially taken aback when our strategies for revitalizing the communities around us, use data, maps, and other "facts" to reinforce old patterns of investment that redline and re-segregate those communities, while proposing to be serving the public good.

Mobilizing people as a force for change requires that we engage each other differently. The fragmentation we see in our country today cannot be solved with strategies that are divisive and unfortunately, too many of us well-meaning advocates have been forces for division without even knowing it. We repeat narratives that undermine our success and the ability of others to see their stake in our work.

The fact of the matter is that on many of the issues facing our communities, the scale of the problems fall well beyond our ability, or any one group, one sector, one organization, one political party, or even a whole community working together to solve them. It will take all of us, working together, making compromises, seeing each other's' point of view and sharing the burden that change requires. Real solutions to any of these large issues will take decades to emerge and implement in any meaningful way. Perhaps most importantly, those solutions will only happen as a result of an extraordinary effort to align community residents, relevant government agencies, public and private institutions, nonprofits, and yes, our corporate and commerce partners. We are in desperate need of adaptive leaders who understand and have the skills to align diverse sets of collaborative partners to match the scale of the problems in front of us and who understand this challenge as inherently about reorganizing systems that are no longer meeting the needs of the world in which we live. I am hoping that this describes you!

What Are We Up Against?

Public will building is tough work – no matter what issues you are trying to advance or systems you are trying to change. This work almost by definition, is tough because of the awesome challenges of needing the make your case at multiple levels, to vastly different audiences – many of whom have different appetites for information, data, rhetorical flair or storytelling. As illustrated in the diagram below, to advance our work, we are often trying to make the case at three levels: (1) to powerful influencers (for example, important community leaders, corporate leaders, policymakers or others who hold powerful sway over important stakeholders); (2) to the institutions in our communities, cities and states who are the gatekeepers of important resources we need to advance our work; and (3) to broad public audiences whose support can help us enable the scale we need to advance strong policies.

Balancing Stakeholder Roles, Perspectives, Needs & Interests

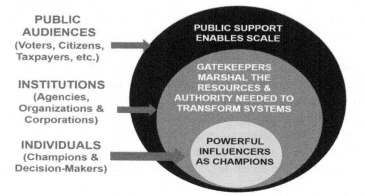

PUBLIC AUDIENCES
(Voters, Citizens, Taxpayers, etc.)

INSTITUTIONS
(Agencies, Organizations & Corporations)

INDIVIDUALS
(Champions & Decision-Makers)

PUBLIC SUPPORT ENABLES SCALE

GATEKEEPERS MARSHAL THE RESOURCES & AUTHORITY NEEDED TO TRANSFORM SYSTEMS

POWERFUL INFLUENCERS AS CHAMPIONS

The outer ring represents our work to make the case to build broader public support and this is the area that often poses the biggest challenge. If our call-to-action is perceived to require any sacrifice or perceived burdens (such as asking for time, tax dollars, support, etc.), we can lose the support we need. This is important because often when we do opinion polling, many people say they are in favor of our ideas — nationalized health care, gun control laws, affordable housing, etc. — are all areas that enjoy broad public support...until our asks become concrete and we share the call-to-action. So, unless we are strategic in how to make the case for these solutions, the values that people say they hold about fixing these problems are mostly theoretical.

It is also, important to say that the audiences at each level have different norms of engagement, appetites for information, data and evidence, as well as varied knowledge about the issues we raise. So, the very nature of making a strong case, when we must do so for vastly different audiences, makes this work inherently challenging.

Yet, the challenge in front of us has become much more difficult in the last 30 years. First, the problems that we are called to solve have gotten much more complex than in previous decades — requiring that we understand much more technical information and can evaluate science and data effectively. Many of the policy issues facing our nation are difficult even for our elected leaders to grasp and it becomes even more difficult when we ask ordinary Americans, who have little time to engage on these issues, to come along with us on the journey. So, the nature of the ask has gotten more cumbersome during this time period. In addition, the technological, political and cultural shifts that have taken place during this time period pose equally compelling challenges.

As such, it has become much harder to engage Americans in a constructive dialogue about promising solutions to the challenges our nation faces and to get their commitment to support those solutions. Some of this difficulty can be blamed on an increasingly toxic culture of political partisanship and polarization. Yet, partisanship and polarization are not the only culprits. There are so many additional issues that limit our ability to pull potential champions of our work forward, that we have to acknowledge and effectively navigate around them so that we get the support our work deserves.

Chief among the challenges we face is the increasing cynicism and lack of confidence that people have in our leaders today. When we add in the misinformation, fake news and alternative facts, it becomes even more difficult for us to counter negative and harmful narratives. Moreover, for those of us working to change systems so that they work better for our communities, that task is made more challenging because few people really understand the systems as they exist today nor do they have any confidence that changing those systems of governance will have any real benefit to their lives. Without the confidence that change is possible and will reap practical benefits for them, they are unlikely to opt out of their bystander status and jump into the fray to help lift up that system change.

The Challenge of Building <u>Public</u> Will

Strong Cultural Narratives (American Dream, Self-Makingness, Racial Difference, Progress, etc.)

Political Partisanship & Social Fragmentation

Cynicism & Lack of Public Confidence in Leaders

Misinterpretation or Skepticism of Data

Misinformation, Fake News & Alternative Facts

System Change? Little Understanding of Governance Systems

Crisis Fatigue & Fear of Carrying the Burden

Scarcity Mindset, Self-Interest, Face at the Bottom

Fear of Change & Path Dependence

Plus, The Challenge of <u>Political</u> Will

Strong Cultural Narratives (American Dream, Self-Makingness, Racial Difference, Progress, etc.)

Policy Advocates Say Everything is a Crisis

Election Cycle & Short Policy Time Horizon

Lobbyists, Wealthy Donors & Influencers Have Outsized Voice

Red Tape and Bureaucracy Protect the Status Quo

Budgets Squeezed by Increasing Expectations

Out-of-Touch with Reality of Most People's Lives

Easier to Ignore Roots Causes

Conquer & Divide Politics Normalized

Building the _public and_ _political will_ necessary to transform the systems that shape the future of our communities, is one of the most critical challenges of our time.

When we think specifically about building political will, a related but slightly different challenge, a set of other issues can be added to this list of hurdles. Many Americans have leaned into a "bystander" stance with respect to public issues for a larger set of reasons — the negativity of the news media that pits people against each other as sports fighters; powerful interests suppressing public participation and activism through voter suppression, gerrymandering, and other mechanisms; and a host of other reasons.

As a result, building public will is not simply a matter of lobbying policymakers, leading influencer campaigns, creating fact sheets to "build awareness", polling to find the "persuadables", or producing the next bleeding-heart commercial whose goal it is to shame us all into action. These activities (which often stand-in for public will building) do not really get at the heart of why people are so disconnected, nor do they provide a framework for understanding how we might reconnect them. So, the work in front of us is to more strategically engage the people in their communities, in our nation and around the world. That is, our real work is to produce an active and informed citizenry that can be a counterweight in shaping the development of the future of our communities, our nation, and planet.

Building public will is about navigating and countering a wide range of impediments to action — challenges that keep people from seeing their stake in the success of collective deliberation and mobilization for better and more inclusive communities.

It takes as its central charge the imperative to get Americans not just engaged but inspired and enthusiastic about the work to be done to redesign the systems that no longer serve to advance the long march toward equity, inclusion and true democracy. It means re-examining why so many Americans are bystanders in their own lives and evaluating the best social science and community practices for putting people back in the front seats.

Our work is to help Americans remember the impulse to "charge the hill", "dump the tea", and "take the state house back". This acknowledges that unless we address the underlying issues at their root, we will not be able to shift the culture of bystander politics and rally the nation toward better solutions.

Public will is the very foundation on which a better future is possible, and we need intentional and strategic efforts to rebuild it. Simply put, there is no way around this; it is broad public support that enables the kind of scale needed to transform systems and enact longer-term, more impactful solutions. Yet, this work often languishes precisely because, it is tough work. Doing this work intentionally, means the proverbial, jumping into the deep end of the pool to make things much better. That is exactly what this Field Guide is designed to help you do.

No matter the specific set of issues animating this bystander culture, for those of us still wanting to improve the communities around us, we have to get better at navigating this set of issues. And too often, we are losing this battle. We are losing not because we don't have a persuasive message, data and statistics. We are losing because we are failing to address the complexity of what's happening in our culture and directly addressing that complexity in our appeals for support.

Perhaps, worst of all, when we fail to make an effective and compelling case for change, our attempts to build public will:

- have unintended and counter-productive effects (the *backfires*)

- result only in small victories (the *backpacks*) or marginal improvements in policy, regulatory, and system reforms, even though we need stronger measures to address these adaptive challenges

- get rejected because people are reacting to our call-to-action out of a belief system they acquired long ago (the *bedtime stories*) rather than to the current facts and statistics we are presenting about what's happening in our communities.

We describe these more fully in the next section.

Navigating the Traps

The lack of broader public support for solutions that could improve our communities and the people in them, should concern us deeply, not just because we need greater support to improve our communities but because our understanding about why we do not enjoy public support is incomplete. An incomplete understanding means that we engage in responses that worsen, rather than improve our ability to engage people. As a result, we often find ourselves losing in the court of public opinion when we try to enact more substantive system reforms.

- **The Backfires.** Too often we let our data and research about the challenges facing our communities, stand-in for a strong call-to-action. And when we do, it often backfires for a variety of reasons. We overestimate the extent to which data, research and evidence can move public support for action. Those data can easily become the negative flash point for people who feel disconnected from these issues more generally, or who disagree with the broader set of solutions we propose. Surely, data are important for designing, implementing and evaluating investments that help our communities, but those data must be embedded in a broader effort to make the case for systems change in an equitable and inclusive way, if they are to be helpful in elevating public support. Moreover, using the wrong data (credentialing the problem rather than the solution)— especially when we are trying to advance equity issues — produces an especially unfortunate backfire that ultimately serves to undermine our work.

   ❧   **The Backpacks.** When we make the case for change, if we fail to frame our concerns as system problems, we risk having our concerns be dismissed, undermined or under-resourced. This is in part because our natural instinct is to solve problems where we see them occur (mostly at the level of individuals or communities) rather than where the roots of those problems may reside (systems). As a result, we get the consolation prizes (small victories or backpacks) when our case for change does not lift up our issues as systems level challenges. While it is true that many of the problems our society faces can and should be solved at multiple levels, we are missing the opportunity to make important system reforms that could make our work more impactful.

   ❧   **The Bedtime Stories.** Our attitudes, opinions, expectations about our lives and the ways we think about the world, were largely shaped as children. Bedtime stories not only put many of us to sleep at night, but they also helped our parents and caregivers convey how the world was supposed to work, the values we should respect and who the "bad guys" were. We may be all grown up today but the basic ideas that characterized our bedtime stories are still with us, structuring how we see the world. When we, as changemakers, fail to recognize the power of those stories in shaping the attitudes of those whose support we hope to gain, we can hopelessly spin-our-wheels trying to talk people out of those old ideas but fail to do so. Our task is not to talk people out of antiquated ideas about the world, as we often try to do, but rather to route people around them. That is, we have to give them new ways to think about issues that do not trigger those old ideas. Putting people in the future is very important because, the future is something we can create together. Carefully rooting people in our shared history, but helping them navigate to the future, is one of the most important techniques of casemaking.

While there are many traps (many of which we discuss later in this Guide), these are the big three (backfires, backpacks and bedtime stories). On almost every issue that requires alignment across many different groups and to forge cross-difference alliances, these are the three that show up universally, no matter what the issue. As a result, if your goal is to engage people effectively and build a groundswell of support, you need to figure out early on — where the backfires are? What are the backpacks that people are willing to sacrifice in lieu of true system change? What are the bedtime stories that they are telling themselves that limit the effectiveness of the case we are making? Once you have mapped those, then you can address the less ominous traps.

We do not wish
or imagine a return
to the way things were.

That's a trap!

We demand that we
emerge to a better
world!

We are forging a new
pathway to a future that
is big enough for all of us
to thrive and prosper!

The Don'ts: Avoid These Responses at All Costs

- 🪱 Myth vs. Fact Sheets (That Focus on the Myths!)

- 🪱 Negatively Framed Data or Data Solely about the Problem

- 🪱 Crisis Stories and Language

- 🪱 The "Clap-Back": Directly Responding to the Negative Disruptors

- 🪱 History Lessons About the Perils of Systems, People or Groups

- 🪱 Villainizing the People, Organizations or Groups that You Need to Change Policy and Systems

- 🪱 Overly Complex Descriptions of Your Work or the Problem

- 🪱 Overly Partisan or Tribalist Perspectives

To avoid these traps, we have to be intentional about making the case. That is, the way we make the case for change matters. Making the case by starting with any of the practices outlined here, is a sure-fire way to get hit with backfires, backpacks and bedtime stories! Of course, the intention behind each of these practices are good ones. They assume that people can be motivated to take action if they understand the issues we care about as: urgent, complex, long-term, large-scale crises that are being exacerbated by bad people, making self-interested and/or bad decisions. Some or all of the latter may be true of the issues on which we are working but the issue is that reminding people of any of these things rarely brings this forward in constructive ways. Rather, what happens more often than not, is that we scare and shame people into bystander status. Who wants to deal with this "mess" after a long day of work!

While fear and shame are powerful motivators, if we are not careful about how we handle and navigate around those emotions for our audiences, they derail our efforts for change. Fear, in particular, won't help you generate the long-term, collaborative support from the stakeholders you need to advance your solutions by itself. You'll need more than that!

And, while it is important that people understand history, have access to data, understand the urgency and the challenges of solving social issues, we have to be thoughtful about HOW we leverage those strategies as part of our call-to-action.

Reflection Question

DON'T RAISE YOUR VOICE, IMPROVE YOUR ARGUMENT.

Desmond Tutu

South African Social Rights Activist and Anglican cleric who in 1984 received the Nobel Prize for Peace for his role in the opposition to apartheid in South Africa.

What is Strategic CaseMaking™

While it is important to present facts as well as to recognize and explain how the policies of the past have had a deleterious impact, history lessons are not proving to be effective mechanisms for building the public will needed to dismantle harmful policies and redesign unjust systems. We need a different approach — one that overcomes impediments to action.

To advance support for policies and programs that need scale, we must do a much better job of navigating the most toxic, dominant narratives or public ways in which people express their support or opposition to policy issues. We must also help people practice telling new narratives of possibility, change and transformation.

Building public will requires us to be more intentional about HOW we make the case for systems change. As leaders, most of us have learned how to present logical arguments with our data and evidence or through the stories of friends, neighbors, co-workers or family who are suffering. Yet these arguments miss the mark when they do not recognize and anticipate how those stories and arguments will be received by public audiences — audiences who already have predisposed beliefs about how the world works.

If our goal is to build public support for deep and transformational system change in our communities and on issues we care about, we will need to redefine what it means to "make the case" for the policies, programs and investments, we know would help.

Our task is to be intentional about how we make the case — at very least to do no harm and at most, change the public conversation in ways that lift up the need for systems change. Below, we define casemaking as the act (really the art and science) of casemaking.

On adaptive challenges this requires us to be explicit about advancing a world that is more equitable and inclusive as well as one where we take collective responsibility for bringing that world into existence. And because adaptive challenges require alignment of a great number of stakeholders and strategic partners, casemaking is literally about the art of aligning people around a course of action (or solution).

case • making
[keys-mey-king]   *noun*

1: the act of making a convincing or persuasive argument about how the world can ought to work to advance equity and the collective responsibility we have to manifest that world through intentional systems change work.

2: enrolling support from key stakeholders in a course of action, a way of thinking, or new belief system by limiting social distance.

A Word about Social Distancing. In early 2020, the COV-19 virus began silently circulating around the world and as everyone is now aware, has now fundamentally changed our lives in ways we never would have imagined. To address the pandemic that resulted, public health officials advised us to socially distance ourselves from each other until the highly infectious virus could run its course. In the middle of a pandemic, physically distancing ourselves from each other is wise counsel but not so in casemaking.

To effectively make the case for systems change, a significant part of our work is to "limit social distance". Let's be clear about what that means. If the case you are making is about affordable rental housing and I am a homeowner, that issue (on the face of it) does not seem like it is relevant to me. I may be in support of affordable housing but it's not really very relevant to me. Similarly, if your case is about opioid addiction and this is not an issue that I nor my family, friends or people in my network seem to face, then as painful as it may be for some, it's not that relevant to me. That is social distance in the context of casemaking.

The goal of casemaking is to help people see their stake in solving these adaptive challenges and we do that by connecting to people more meaningfully. The principles of Strategic CaseMaking™ outlined in this Guide are meant to help you powerfully connect people's lives, ambitions, hopes, dreams and even their fears, to the issues in your case. The more they see OUR issues as THEIR issues (limited social distance), the more effective our call-to-action will be.

So, stay "physically" distant as our nation adjusts to the world where infectious viruses are an ongoing threat but learn the art and science of pulling people closer and connecting them to the adaptive challenges that are important for us to solve. That skills set, is the very essence of Strategic CaseMaking™.

So, **Strategic CaseMaking**™ works to bring our stakeholders closer to the issues we are trying to solve (limiting their social distance) and reinforces how they benefit from helping to resolve issues that they may not perceive as affecting them. This is critical to our ability to build public will — if we do not or cannot build a sense of connection between our stakeholders and the issues we raise, it sets us up for backfires, marginal results and missed opportunities.

Strategic CaseMaking™ is not a magic bullet and even at its best, will not help us convince everybody. Yet, it can help us reshape the public conversation so that those whose opinions can be redirected, will be. And although we won't win over everybody or all potential stakeholders with a more thoughtful casemaking approach, we HAVE TO win over some of them.

In this way, casemaking is about changing the way that we invite a more thoughtful public discourse, how we help people see their stake in our success and how we ultimately, bring a broader sense of trust, belonging and agency to the issues we are trying to solve.

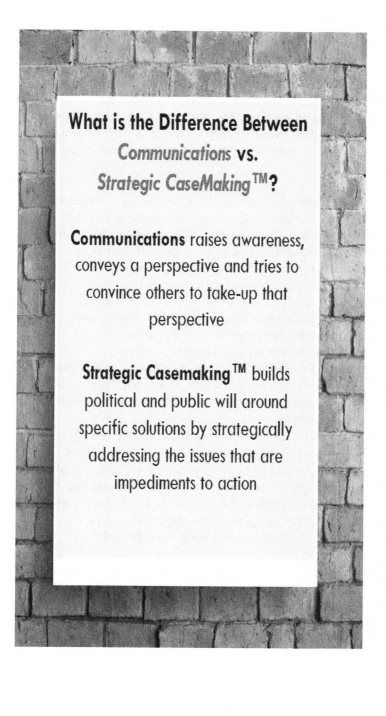

When deployed effectively, Strategic CaseMaking™ can be instrumental in building stronger public support for our work by reducing the social distance or disconnection they feel from the issues we are raising as leaders and changemakers. This is a part of what distinguishes casemaking from communications, more generally.

Communications is generally about raising awareness of key issues and trying to convince people to take-up a viewpoint or understanding. CaseMaking is related but very different. Casemaking focuses on addressing the impediments to action that often keep people from leaning forward on issues that need their participation. For example, when people are as polarized and distrustful as they are in the current environment, it often means that our messaging is rejected by important stakeholders without consideration. Once they know something about our political affiliation for example, they may "distance" themselves or reject our call-to-action so, it becomes harder to mobilize them. Casemaking is about recognizing things like partisanship (or any other category of difference) as a potential impediment and crafting ways to make the case for change that overcome it. We overcome this kind of impediment, not simply by extolling the virtues of the solutions we propose, but by using the best social science to circumnavigate that polarization and distrust.

Unfortunately, there are lots of impediments to action, so we have our work cut out for us, no matter what our case is about. The purpose of this Guide is to change those dynamics in our favor, using the best social science and community building evidence available!

The Social Science Behind the Approach

So finally, here is the good news! There really is an art and a science that we can use to limit social distance, pull people closer to the adaptive solutions that matter most, and get the groundswell of support we need to equitably and inclusively make our systems work better. In particular, there is a growing body of social science and emergent strategies from community development practitioners that can inform and strengthen how we make the case for systems change.

Strategic CaseMaking™ is a synthesis of the most powerful of those strategies. The approach outlined here is empirically based, time-tested and practical. This framework is interdisciplinary — drawing extensively from across the social sciences.

> *We are, as a species,*
> *addicted to story. Even*
> *when the body goes to sleep,*
> *the mind stays up all night,*
> *telling itself stories.*
>
> *Jonathan Gottschall, Author*
> *The Storytelling Animal: How Stories Make Us Human*

The first and most foundational part of the evidence-base we draw from, comes from the science behind powerful and compelling storytelling. Storytelling has become the subject of a great many books and scientific studies. We know that when people hear new information in the form of stories, they listen differently. They digest that information more effectively and our stories help us to convey ideas that deeply engage people's emotion, empathy and inclination for action.

Powerful storytelling can advance our cause far beyond any data point or press release. But to be effective at helping people see the benefit of equity, inclusion and system change, our stories have to be told strategically. And this is where the full spectrum of social science becomes helpful.

We have to become practiced at telling stories that not only inform people about the adaptive challenges we face but that inspire them to action. We have to tell stories that underscore the value and benefit of planning, system building and restoration. We have to tell stories with and about people who are directly affected by the success and failure of those systems. And we have to tell stories that help us to be honest and authentic about the harm and trauma caused to so many people because our institutions ground them down.

One way to think of the principles of casemaking outlined in this Guide is as a storytelling guide. Principles that when woven together, helps us to deeply improve our storytelling for systems change. Stories that help people see the adaptive challenges we face as deeply connected to their own aspirations and thus, requiring their urgency. Stories that allow us to see our collective stake and responsibility for the success of solutions on the table. Stories that help us to clearly assess the advantages of urgent and thoughtful action versus the consequences of inaction. Stories that help us remain accountable for the promises we make to each other and those that help us use our data to understand why our investments in each other matter. Stories that remind us of our past triumphs and the times we acted in unison as our better angels. Stories that make us feel another, more equitable world is possible and that makes each of us feel like our collective contributions are the ones that matter most. Stories that remind us that "government" is nothing but a collection of people (with the same faults and short-sightedness that we all have), trying to organize the world for the better.

Do the Groundwork:
Frame the Adaptive Challenge Before You Begin CaseMaking

One of the biggest mistakes that leaders make is they fail to nail down and communicate the adaptive challenge that they are trying to solve. That is, what is the real challenge that needs to be solved. Often, the thing that they are fighting about or advocating for, isn't actually the problem that needs to be solved. That's why we named our framework STRATEGIC CaseMaking because it is fundamentally about being strategic and that means bringing clarity to the thing we are actually working to solve. Too often, leaders are chasing down facts and figures about policy issues without even recognizing that what's really going on in terms of the reluctance of others to follow our call-to-action, has little to do with the policy, programs or services we are working to save or implement. It is also the case that they don't understand the bigger picture and so the urgency or scale of what we're trying to do, simply doesn't register.

So, before any work begins to make your case, take the time to figure out what the adaptive challenge is that you are really working toward. Start out by asking, if the world is changing rapidly and we will need to be prepared for the next millennia, how will this [issue, policy, program, service, or investment], help us to be prepared for it? Why do we need to address this issue to have a bright future? How will our call-to-action help us to prepare for the world that is coming, for the economy that is coming, for the demographic and technological shifts that are coming, and for the planet we will inherit? Whatever your answers to those questions are, that is how you start to define what's the adaptive challenge in front of you.

An Example: School Desegregation Policy

Take for example a school district taking up the need for redistricting to balance student population and to address equity issues across the community. Increasingly, this issue is a more common source of tension where community members fight each other over what the school rezoning or redistricting policy should be. The public conversation might be outwardly about the redistricting policy, but the underlying adaptive challenge is about better serving the needs of all students and doing so in an equitable fashion.

We all espouse the value of equity, but we have not been very successful in helping our institutions to figure out how they implement and embed those values in action. If we choose to fight the policy issue, and not identify the adaptive challenge, it becomes even more difficult to bring our stakeholders and strategic partners to the table to resolve this issue thoughtfully.

Why is that an adaptive challenge? Simply put, as calls for the social goals around equity are increasing, we are putting more pressure on institutions of all kinds to operationalize our values of equity. Schools are a primary place where inequities are fundamentally built into the fabric of policy, so they have become ground zero for many in operationalizing our values around equity. So, the adaptive challenge is not busing policy *per se* — it is how do we operationalize our expectations, societal goals and values around equity? That's the core issue. Our task is to help people fully get that equity is important, that they have a stake in this goal and that they actually benefit more by choosing to advance equity than by trying to fit it.

It is important as we frame the adaptive challenge, to also be clear about what would happen if we fail to solve that challenge and why that failure would spell disaster for ALL of us — not just the students who will not have access to the quality of educational resources that gives them better odds of long-term success.

- **The adaptive challenge in this example:** *operationalize equity and improve educational outcomes so that we are all prepared for the economy that is coming; a world that will value diversity of experiences, skills set, cultural fluency, and more.*

- **If we fail to solve this challenge:** *we simply will not have the kind of skilled workforce or citizenry that we need to remain competitive in a more globalized economy; we also will take our history of social, economic and racial inequity into the future; we reinforce and potentially even exacerbate the inequity in this community.*

- **This matters for everybody in this region because:** *communities and regions rise or they fall together; at a time when we need all-hands-on-deck to prepare for the economy that is coming, we must drive policies that help us grow the capacity of the young people in whose care we will place the institutions that we have created in this community.*

An Example: Community Health Worker Programs
For something like community health programs, which are notoriously under-resourced, the adaptive challenge is slightly different. The challenge is not that those programs need more funding (that is the symptom of a bigger adaptive challenge). The challenge is that we have raised our expectations, goals and values around health equity and population outcomes.

We know that many of the people who most need medical care and to access health resources are not likely to receive those resources through traditional health facilities. As a result, our ability to reach those populations and serve them effectively, as well as our ability to bring down their health care costs, require a different approach. So, the adaptive challenge is not really about the community health programs themselves, they are one means to a bigger end.

- **The adaptive challenge in this example:** *operationalizing equity and improving health outcomes in the context of our community health resource allocation process.*

- **If we fail to solve this challenge:** *many of the people who live and work in this community will not have the medical care they need and the costs to care for them down the road will be much higher for all of us; also, we take a history of social, economic and racial inequity into the future, continuing the practices that led up to a health care system that is out of reach for many; we reinforce and potentially even exacerbate the inequity that has plagued this community for decades.*

- **This matters for everybody in this region because:** *at a time when our health care needs are changing and the costs of care are rising steeply, we need new models of care that meet people where they are and allow our system to more adequately serve people in this community; we need all-hands-on-deck to prepare for the new public health threats that are coming; we lose the productive capacity of a great number of people who could be contributing to our future.*

The benefit of taking the time to frame the adaptive challenge is that we get super clear on: what the problem is that we're trying to solve, why it matters that we solve it, why it benefits everybody that we solve it, and what the consequences of inaction are — BEFORE WE TRY TO MAKE THAT CASE TO ANYBODY ELSE!

This phase of your work is also important because it helps set up the forward-thinking, productive mindset needed to craft a credible case for support and to motivate the people you need to hear and heed your call-to-action.

In your case, you'll need to frame the two tomorrows for people: one where we adapt to a more equitable and inclusive future or one where we bring the old inequities and divisiveness forward. One of those tomorrows leaves our cities, our communities, our planet and our people barren. The other offers up the possibility of an evergreen planet and people who are thriving. That's the adaptive challenge in front of us, so be clear on how the work that you are doing contributes to the latter!

Take the time to do this groundwork first and to paint those two tomorrows very clearly. Either we rise to the occasion of this adaptive challenge and plan for the needs of this community or we choose to be divided, unprepared, and at risk of the uncertainty of any future shocks. Those are the choices and the stories that you create as part of your casemaking needs to fully help people to understand the starkness of those choices.

When you are clear on what the adaptive challenge is and you can help others be clear on what that challenge is, it will infinitely strengthen how you make your case. As the old adage goes, clarity is kindness! And as a practical matter, it helps you more fully develop the story that will flow as part of the case you are making.

The complex adaptive challenges our nation faces can only be solved when we work to align a great number of people, institutions, agencies, organizations, houses of worship, and corporate partners. All of whom have different attitudes, beliefs, perspectives, biases and interests.

We either rise to the occasion to create a world that works for all and that is evergreen, or we become bystanders to our own failure.

That's why it's tough!
That's the work!

Do the Groundwork First:
Take the Time to Put the Big Rocks In

Business consultants often spout the adage — *put the big rocks in first*. They usually say this to try to get their clients to prioritize and focus chiefly on the things that matter most. Well in this case, what is true for business consultants, is also a useful adage for those of us making the case for change. Before you start to make your case, take the time to define the big rocks that make it possible for people to open themselves up to the possibility of your argument.

No matter who the particular stakeholders or strategic partners that you are making your case to, they need to:

- **trust** you and the validity of the case you are making

- feel that they **belong** to the group of people for which you are advocating or trying to help (belonging is powerful) and feel a sense of agency (or empowerment) to act

- perceive that they have a **stake** in your success or will benefit from it

- know that you have listened to them and **understand their experiences**

- **understand what role they play** in your success

- believe that there is added power in <u>working with you</u> (collectively efficacy) and your solution has the potential to actually work.

These big rocks are the building blocks on which your case will be built. The most important of these are trust, belonging and stake. If you miss the opportunity to position these big rocks first, it will greatly diminish your ability to make your case. And ultimately, it is unlikely that you will be able to get the support you need from your stakeholders and gain the support of new champions of your work.

People often assume away these big rocks, but it is worth the time and energy to first make sure that you have the trust of the people you are talking to. If you haven't already established a working relationship with the people you are talking to — prioritize this work first. Spend time with people, engage in active listening, take note of how they talk about their pain points and aspirations. Try to see the world from their perspective and imagine what would inspire you if you were in their shoes. Do not underestimate how much time this foundational work takes.

Trust takes time to build and there are few accelerators to advance you without putting in the work here. Putting the big rocks in first means establishing the connections and relationships that enable a strong case to be made.

Reflection
Question

Have I done all that I can to ensure that my stakeholders feel a sense of belonging, trust, stake, shared experience, and confidence in our collaborative action? Do they understand their role in our success?

10 Core Principles of Strategic CaseMaking™

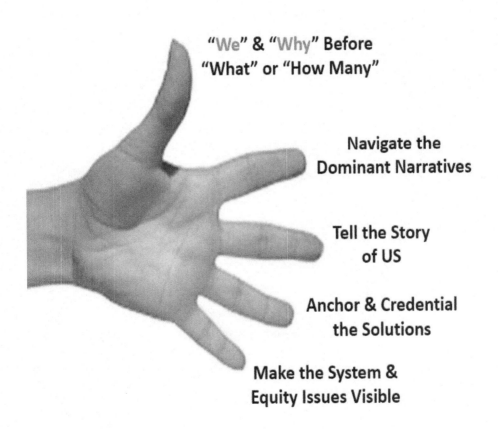

"We" & "Why" Before "What" or "How Many"

Navigate the Dominant Narratives

Tell the Story of US

Anchor & Credential the Solutions

Make the System & Equity Issues Visible

To start reaping the benefits of a Strategic CaseMaking™ approach, use the principles we outline here. You don't have to master all of them at once but start with the We/Why and keep working from there.

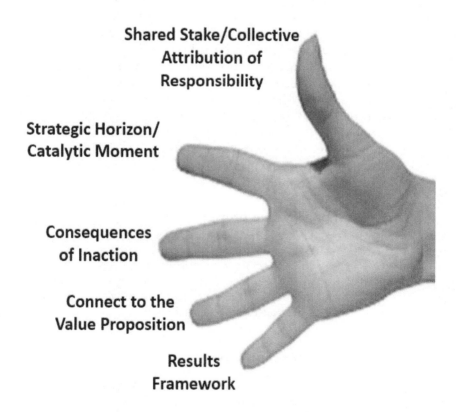

Shared Stake/Collective
Attribution of
Responsibility

Strategic Horizon/
Catalytic Moment

Consequences
of Inaction

Connect to the
Value Proposition

Results
Framework

Deploying the Principles

Putting the principles to work is the focus of this section of the Guide. In the pages that follow, each principle is described, and resources are provided to deploy that principle in your materials. Be clear though, the intention is not that you'll be able to "plug in" a few new words that will magically persuade your stakeholders and strategic partners to take the action that you've proposed (that would be a totally unrealistic expectation). The goal here however is to provide useful tools and resources that can be used as helpful inputs to improve the case for change that you are making (in proposals, pitch decks, presentations and other externally facing materials). As you practice them, you will be better able to apply them in whatever context you are working.

For each principle we provide the following tools.

What's the Principle?

Each principle is described so that you understand what the principle is, the context for it, why it matters, how it works and how to deploy it in your materials to make the case.

Reflection Questions

After the description of each principle, reflection questions are offered so that you can start to ask the questions that help you to strengthen how you are making the case. Use these questions to lead conversations with your team, allies, board, and other champions of your efforts.

Tickets to Success & Pro-Tips

Here we provide expert tools, tips, and guides that can help you make the best use of that principle. These two sections provide your "ticket" to better practice gleaned from real world experience across a variety of issue areas as well as pro-tips.

Sample Success Metrics

Casemaking can take multiple tries to bring new strategic partners along. How do you know when you've effectively deployed a principle in your case? You'll know because you can benchmark your performance with a few sample metrics that can be useful bellwethers along the way, to help you know if we're on the right track and to mark your progress along the way.

Examples and Sample Language

We share specific language examples from real campaigns, proposals, pitch decks, and other materials that we've worked on over the years. We've changed the names and some of the information in the examples (since some of the materials are proprietary or confidential). But the goal here is to show how the principles can be deployed effectively across from different issue areas, sectors, institutional contexts, and messengers. Again, this is not "plug and play" language but rather, examples provided so that you can get a sense of what the principle looks like in a real context. Full case studies can be found on our website (www.TheCaseMade.com).

Be flexible, but stick to your principles.

Eleanor Roosevelt
*Diplomat, Activist, and Longest
Serving First Lady of the United States*

Principle #1: Start by Establishing the "We" and Wrap It Around A Strong, Shared "Why"

Making an effective case means speaking first to the aspirations of the people to whom we are talking. When we lift up people's core aspirations for THEIR lives, work or community, they are more willing to hear us, even when the conversations that we need to have with them are tough or require some sacrifice on their part. This means that the success of the case we are making depends in part on our understanding the values that motivate the folks we are talking to (their WHY) and our ability to articulate how those values are shared (our WE). When we open the conversation by connecting those two (WE and WHY), we lay the foundation for our casemaking and opening of a story that grabs people's attention. People are much more likely to listen to our point of view when they believe we share the same values and the same animating concerns (WHY).

Establishing the WE and WHY first, provides your stakeholders with a sense of belonging and opens the opportunity for collective problem-solving. When we fail to establish a strong sense of, WE and WHY as the lead to the case that we are making, we don't have a strong foundation for engaging their support. So, take the time to listen to and incorporate the aspirations of the people you are making your case to, before ANYTHING else you want to convey.

The Strategic CaseMaking™ Blueprint

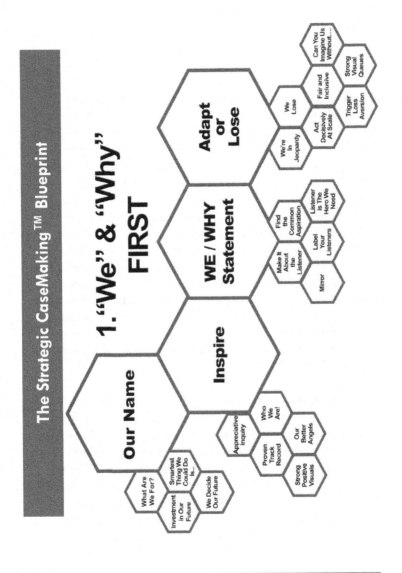

1. "We" & "Why" FIRST

Our Name

- What Are We For?
- Smartest Thing We Could Do Is...
- Investment in Our Future
- We Decide Our Future

Inspire

- Appreciative Inquiry
- Who We Are!
- Proven Track Record
- Our Better Angels
- Strong Positive Visuals

WE / WHY Statement

- Find the Common Aspiration
- Listener Is The Hero We Need
- Make It About the Listener
- Label Your Listeners
- Mirror

Adapt or Lose

- We're In Jeopardy
- We Lose
- Can You Imagine Us Without....
- Act Decisively At Scale
- Fair and Inclusive
- Strong Visual Queues
- Trigger Loss Aversion

Reflection Questions

☐ Have I identified shared values that speak to the aspirations of the stakeholders hearing my case?

☐ Have I opened the conversation by relating those shared values (WHY) to the issues and solutions that I am proposing?

☐ Have I established a sense of WE (a positive collective identity) that can help position my stakeholders with enough stake and standing to problem-solve together?

Your Ticket to Implementing This Principle

There are many ways to get the information you need to advance this principle in your work. Skilled negotiators often use the practice of mirroring. So, instead of creating your own language at the top of your message, mirror the positive language at the top of THEIR recent messages and then connect it in an appreciative way to the work that you are doing. In this way, you are helping your stakeholders to make the connection between their WHY and yours!

Sample Success Measures

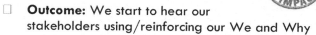
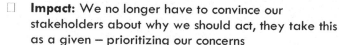

☐ **KPI:** We are consistently starting our messaging by articulating our WE and WHY

☐ **Outcome:** We start to hear our stakeholders using/reinforcing our We and Why

☐ **Impact:** We no longer have to convince our stakeholders about why we should act, they take this as a given – prioritizing our concerns

ASSET-BASED FRAMING AND APPRECIATIVE INQUIRY

At the most basic level, asset-based framing and appreciative Inquiry are twin processes. Asset based framing in the context of casemaking is about engaging people and their communities through their aspirations and contributions before any conversation about their problems, challenges or the "deficits" that exist in the environments around them. Asset-framing assumes that communities had value <u>before</u> the nonprofit showed up, or that kids have value even <u>before</u> and <u>after</u> the take standardized tests, no matter their score. It means refusing to label people as "at-risk" or characterizing them as "homeless" and then having a discussion about the problems they face.

So much of the framing in the case we make to advance system change, begins with negative framing of the very people and places we are trying to help. This kind of framing dooms our work from the very beginning - defining the conversation by pointing to major problems that often demoralizes the very people that we are working so hard to mobilize.

When we open the conversation with asset-based framing instead, we change the energy in the conversation and enable people to operate from a position of strength rather than their faults. Starting by defining ourselves as innovators, pioneers, good neighbors, etc., and giving examples of when we have exhibited that behavior, sets the tone of the conversation and gives people the goal to live into.

To deepen this sense of strength, we ask follow-up questions from a place of appreciative inquiry. Appreciative inquiry is the art of asking unconditional, positive questions to strengthen people's capacity to anticipate and look forward to solving hard challenges — which is ultimately what we want them to do.

When we ask questions that appreciate who people already are (asset-based framing) and then ask questions from the vantage point of appreciation (appreciative inquiry), we change the energy of the entire conversation and open people up for the tough work that follows.

The following summarizes how appreciative inquiry questions are different:

- The questions we ask, almost always determine the answers we get. Essentially, we live in the world our questions create.

- The more positive our questions, the easier it will be for us to conceive of positive and constructive outcomes.

- When we ask people to answer questions from a position of strength, we give them the opening and space to be the hero of our story. Ultimately, that's what helps people to see value in their joining our call-to-action

- Our questions create the space for movement and change, if we ask them right. They should open up the space for people to reconsider their prior disposition – not because they were wrong, but because WE HAVE THE OPPORTUNITY to create something really great together! If our goal is to prove or make others wrong, we remove the incentive and space for self-reflection and correction.

This may seem counter-intuitive, but few people like to admit that they may have made an error in judgement and you starting there is unlikely to win the support you need to advance your work.

Below are some foundational appreciative inquiry questions for a variety of situations in which you are likely to be making a case. They are meant to be general examples but feel free to tailor ones that best reflect the uniqueness of your stakeholders and the context in which you are working.

For People:
- What has been a high-point experience in your life when you felt most alive, successful, and effective?

- Without being humble, what do you value most about yourself, your work, and your organization?

- What can you continue doing to keep amplifying the good in your life and with people around you?

- What are the assets you bring or contribute to this community, city or the region?

For Organizations:

- What are the core factors that make this organization function at its best, when it feels like a great place to be in, and without which it would cease to exist?

- Imagine it is three years into the future and the organization is just as you would want it to be. What's happening that makes it vibrant and successful? What has changed? What has stayed the same, and how have you contributed to this future?

- What can you begin to do to move the organization in the direction of our greatest desires? What can you stop doing because it no longer serves the organization or gets in the way?

- What are some transitions you'll need to make because you have existing responsibilities and constraints, and can't just drop everything immediately?

- What is the part of the organizational theory of change / action that inspires you? How does your work in this organization and the expertise that you bring contribute to the heart of this organization?

For Communities:

- When you think about the future of this city and your neighborhood in particular, what are you most optimistic about?

- You could live anywhere in the world or in the country, what makes you love this community? Not the parks and weather or cultural things like zoos, but other things that are really unique about this community that makes you excited to be here, even on a tough day?

- Have you been here long enough to remember when the people in this community were able to overcome a major issue? How did that happen? What made that successful?

- Wow, that's amazing! Sounds like people here have a proven track record of tackling tough problems and winning! How does it make you feel to know that people in this community overcame such a challenging issue in the past?

- Why do you think this is the right and perfect moment to be coming together to improve this community and address whatever challenges exist here?

- How can we take advantage of the opportunity in front of us to make this region/city/community better for everybody?

- As we look to make investments in our future, what do you think is the smartest investment we can make to improve this community?

- Since we decide our future, what decisions are you ready to make to improve this community!

The Smartest Investment We Can Make in Our Town's Future, is To Secure a Foundation of Strong Communities and Stable Homes.

Our Town is comprised of vibrant neighborhoods and a dynamic economy—built on livability and affordability—that gives us a strong competitive advantage, across the state and nationally. Our local businesses attract dedicated employees, our colleges recruit high-caliber talent, and our neighborhoods boast strong and welcoming communities.

This is a critical time to be investing in Our Town. Our Town is one of the few remaining places where housing remains relatively affordable in the state. The favorable Interest rates remain relatively low and growth prospects for the region are optimistic.

Expanding homeownership opportunities to more households across Our Town, not only helps more households build wealth but it enables mortgage lenders to redress redlining and other discriminatory practices that have stained the credibility of the finance industry for decades.

If we act now, we can stop the displacement that threatens to upend whole neighborhoods in Our Town - making it difficult for families to stay connected to the jobs, schools, community centers, arts and cultural events that they have come to love. No one thrives if we price out young adults who have the talent and skills to strengthen our businesses.

No one thrives if businesses leave Our Town because they can't attract and retain a workforce. No one thrives if families struggle to put a roof over their heads.

But we all thrive when people who work here, have stable homes here. We all thrive when our work to bring more businesses and prosperity to Our Town, includes everybody. We all thrive when people see a future here and can raise their families stably here or start new business ventures here.

The more people succeed in Our Town, the more we lay the foundation for Our Town's future. We all have a stake in the success and stability of the neighborhoods that make up Our Town. They are the lifeblood and central arteries of our community. They fuel the engine of our economy. They nurture the diversity of our people and provide outlets to share culture, food, parks, festivals and more.

The neighborhoods in Our Town ensure our future – yours and mine! The smartest investment we could make together is uniting in policies that strengthen all neighborhoods. Every home, in every neighborhood should be a place where possibility, hopefulness, and opportunity thrive. We will make Our Town better-block-by-block. Leaving the old practices of exclusion behind and leaning into laying a new foundation for strong and stable homes in every neighborhood in Our Town. Nothing less will do, because we have decided that we can do better!

Principle #2: Navigate the Dominant Narratives and Negative Disruptors

It would be so much easier to make our case if our stakeholders were blank slates (without existing opinions, perceptions, stereotypes and biases). Unfortunately, this is not the circumstance we face. More often than not, our stakeholders have already formed opinions about the issues we are trying to solve, opinions about the relevance and importance of those issues, as well as judgements about the deservedness of the people they think will benefit from our solutions.

While some of those preexisting beliefs are constructive, the narratives that tend to dominate our popular culture are usually unhelpful. Our task is not to try to talk people out of these dominant narratives — that strategy is rarely successful and usually backfires (pushing people more staunchly in support of stereotyped beliefs and biases). Making our case requires us to carefully reframe the conversation — pivoting to more productive ways of thinking about the issue. For example, a conversation that might have been about affordable housing or addressing disparities in health, becomes a conversation about ensuring that our zip codes do not determine our access to a better life. We are essentially getting at the same problems, but people may not have the same defenses up or pre-existing stereotypes about zip codes as they do about affordable housing or health disparities. That 's our work in Principle #2.

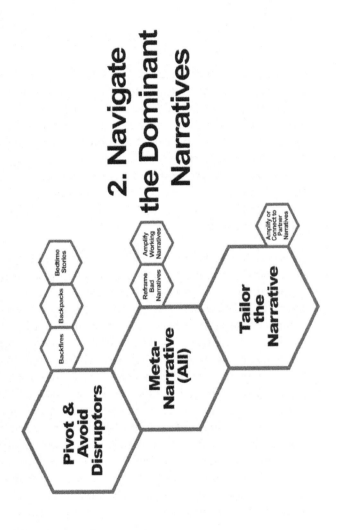

2. Navigate the Dominant Narratives

Pivot & Avoid Disruptors
- Backfires
- Backpacks
- Bedtime Stories

Meta-Narrative (All)
- Reframe Bad Narratives
- Amplify Working Narratives

Tailor the Narrative
- Amplify or Connect to Partner Narratives

Reflection Questions:

- ☐ Have I identified the preexisting beliefs and dominant narratives that shape public opinion about my issue?
- ☐ Have I avoided triggering the dominant narratives that reduce support for the case I am making about that issue?
- ☐ Am I reframing the conversation and amplifying alternative narratives that can help me better connect to my stakeholders?

Your Ticket to Implementing This Principle

Your task is to skillfully navigate around the dominant narratives. Opening the conversation with something your stakeholders appreciate, may help you open the door to the conversation you want to have. You are not trying to change the subject or avoid tackling the biases you see, but by pivoting first, you are buying yourself some time by getting people who would otherwise easily avoid the conversation, to listen. Think of it as "relabeling" – the same practice that designer retailers use when they want you to buy something that was once objectionable to you when it was priced 100x over cost! If they can do it, so can you!

Sample Success Measures

- ☐ **KPI:** We are consistently pivoting away from the dominant narratives to ones that avoid harmful backfires
- ☐ **Outcome:** Our stakeholders are using/reinforcing our new narratives & engaging less in stereotypical/biased conversations on this issue
- ☐ **Impact:** We have unseated the dominance of harmful narratives associated with this issue, in favor or more positive ones

---

THE ART OF AN
EFFECTIVE PIVOT

"That's an interesting question, but there's a bigger issue for us on the table that we should consider . . ."

The ability to pivot from the conversation on the table to the one you want to have, is one of the most important casemaking techniques to have in your toolbelt. If you've ever watched two good debaters go at it, I'm sure you've seen the fine art of an effective pivot. To pivot literally means to take a conversation topic that might be on a specific subject and move it to answer it on your own terms. That is, shifting the conversation back to a frame or a storyline that is consistent with the case that you are making. Think of this casemaking technique as helping your stakeholders and strategic partners stay focused on the mission, stay focused on what's important, stay focused on your call-to-action.

Pivots are a critical part of casemaking efforts because no matter how thoughtful we are in crafting our case, dominant narratives and negative disruptors are commonplace. Dominant narratives are common societal narratives that reinforce ways of thinking that make it more difficult for people to see their collective interest in having systems designed for equity. For example, someone might say, *"yes I know that people need health care insurance, but they should get a job or figure out how to get health insurance on their own."*

What is the Difference Between
Dominant Narratives and
Negative Disruptors?

Dominant Narratives are common explanations, beliefs or ways of thinking that get reinforced through culture (*i.e. through the stories we tell and our cultural norms*) that make it more difficult for people to see their collective interest in having systems designed to produce equitable outcomes. Because dominant narratives are so normalized through their repetition and authority, they have the illusion of being objective and apolitical, when in fact they are neither.

Negative Disruptors often function like dominant narratives in that they can disrupt calls for collection action around equity and they get circulated through culture. What distinguishes negative disruptors is that they are not tightly held beliefs but rather, they are *statements of resignation* about the possibility of change. When people start to plan on the future they aspire to, negative disruptors function as reminders that social change is impossible, the battle for equity is a fool's errand and selective examples of how/when our past efforts to create social change have failed.

That's the dominant narrative of individual responsibility talking and because of the repetition through which it is retold, that kind of narrative is hard to overcome for those trying to advance new policy models for nationalized health care.

Similarly, negative disruptors are equally harmful to our casemaking. Negative disruptors are those statements of resignation that can deflate people's excitement about leaning forward. For example, a typical disruptor in conversations about policy responses to homelessness often looks like this, *"those people are all drug addicts and they'll never be able to be positive contributors to our community."* This person may not be trying to enroll you in a belief system, but the comment is meant to dampen any bright ideas that you might have about creating new policies, programs, services or investments for people experiencing homelessness. No matter what issue you are talking about, there will always be negative disruptors or statements made with the explicit purpose to shut down the aspiration to find better solutions. We have to be strategic to work around them!

If our goal is to make a powerful case, we'll have to keep our stakeholders and strategic partners on course. That means, we have to master the fine art of the pivot. Take the dominant narrative or negative disruptors that you've been handed and turn that conversation right back around to the issues that you know matter. The better your "pivot" strategy, the more likely you are to keep your audience focused. We've all engaged in the pivot at one point, whether we realize it or not. The good news is that there are examples everywhere — from the board room in business, to politics on the cable news channels, to your loved ones at home. Here's an example from my personal collection!

Me (to my 11-year-old son):
   "Hey buddy, have you done your homework?"
My son:
   "Hey mom, I love you so much. What's for dinner?"

Who can argue with a kid that starts a sentence with "I love you"! His homework did get done but he managed to buy himself some time with that one. Some pivots are more effective than others but let's be clear, our ability to pivot determines a large part of how we're received.

Take the case of Lance Armstrong when asked about using drugs to enhance his performance in competitive cycling. Though it didn't come in the form of an interview, interviewers were talking for years about his almost supernatural performance on the bike.

Interviewers to Lance Armstrong:
   "What are you on?"
Lance Armstrong reply via his Nike Commercial:
   "What am I on? I'm on my bike busting my ass six hours a day. What are you on?"

Armstrong was able to use humor and a bit of bravado to push back on claims that tarnished his image (although we should note that eventually those claims were found to be true)! The point here is that he was able to pivot to the conversation HE WANTED TO HAVE, which was about the sport he loved and how hard he was working to stay relevant in it.

As with everything else in this world, pivots can take both good and bad forms—and are put into play for strategic reasons. But how often have you been in a situation where you wanted to have a productive conversation about an issue but the people you were talking to were stuck in another frame? Or they were pushing back on your ideas using narratives that were totally unhelpful, misinformation or "alternative facts" – possibly even, lies? Or perhaps, they were stuck in a bedtime story (as we defined it earlier in this Guide) and they weren't able to hear your position because they couldn't shake their own pre-conceived notions?

There are indeed some people for whom, having you share your facts, data and evidence to the contrary helps them to see your point of view. Unfortunately, it is more often the situation that you'll have to either navigate around those unproductive perceptions or simply acknowledge what you have in common and pivot back to safer territory. So, mastering the fine art of pivoting is essential.

The good news is that the dominant narratives and negative disruptors are usually pretty predictable –

rarely are people creative enough or interested enough to come up with entirely new disruptive things to say every time they meet you! Their lack of creativity and predictability gives us the opportunity to develop (and practice) a standard way that we'll pivot around the issues they raise.

Here are a couple ground rules about effective pivoting.

(1) *NEVER, EVER repeat back the unproductive information – even to clarify.* When you repeat back the negative things you've heard, you simply give your audience another opportunity to hear the other point of view...again! Refuse to entertain the unproductive information – especially if it reinforces dominant narrative, negative stereotypes, bias or bigotry.

(2) *Don't spend much time trying to refute negative narratives or bogus claims/disruptors either.* Because most negative disruptors are almost never the real issue for people (they are more likely defensive shields that people throw up to protect themselves against the idea of change, the imperative to act, etc.), it isn't a good use of your time and it rarely helps. You are on stronger ground if you go back to your own narrative, reinforce the values that you are upholding and work to educate people who are receptive (new champions) about why your solution is the best course of action for our

future.

(3) *Learn the difference between a defensive pivot and an offensive one.* There are two kinds of pivots —the goal of one version is to defend ourselves against unfair or untrue characterizations (defensive) while the goal of the second one is to actively move the conversation away from oppositional narratives and back onto ones that are more productive (offensive). Practice using both so that when you're hit with a negative disruptor, you already know how to make the play (defensively or offensively) that allows you to get back to your own casemaking.

(4) *Instead, use bridging statements to find something that you can agree about and then, get back to your own narrative.* So, the best pivots tend to be those where you acknowledge something in common or some part of the other person's statement that you agree with, and then move back onto your narrative or frame. You are not required to agree with their arguments, but you can always find that one small idea, concern or nugget that you share in common. You might share your concern with the health of the community, or the accountability to our systems, or the wellbeing of our seniors. If that's all you can muster, go to those kinds of themes first.

Some examples of bridging statements:

- *"I share your concern for our community, that's why I believe..."*
- *"Yes, about 10 years ago I would have said the same thing but here's what changed how I see this..."*
- *"Thank you for saying that, it reminds me that..."*
- *"I can see how you could come to that opinion given your concerns, but the bottom line is that..."*
- *"You put a number of important issues on the table but what it all comes down to is this...."*
- *"Well I remember that happening as well, but my recollection suggests that...."*
- *"Yes, you've given a lot of information. What people really need to know though is that..."*
- *"Yes, those are important concerns, but we find the more troubling concern has to do with..."*

(5) *Practice the way that you'll pivot with others so that there is consistency in the alternative direction that you are setting.* Given that you are not the only ones likely facing the same kinds of negative disruptors, work out a consistent way that you (and others responding on the issue) will pivot. Develop and practice a consistent pivot with other advocates so that

together you begin to rewrite the story, change the narrative and rewrite the way that people see the issue over time.

Here's an example of a good pivot: When he was campaigning for health care reform, President Barack Obama and his team made a number of strategic pivots to navigate around the negative disruptors in the public debate. Opposers of the legislation argued that people would lose their ability to choose their own physician as well as access to their existing health plans.

President Obama's pivot looked like this: *"If you like your health care plan, you can keep your health care plan. But under this plan, those same insurers will never be able to deny you coverage for a pre-existing condition if you change plans."* First, he acknowledged something he could agree with and then, Obama would talk excitedly about pre-existing conditions – an issue where public support was rock solid, so he knew he was on solid ground. If you want to advance a strong case for change, master the art of the pivot and get to solid ground. Caucus with others who are actively advocating on the issues you care about and work together on the specific pivots that will help you circle back to solid ground. That's the way to keep people focused on the story you are telling.

TRY ME! The dominant narratives and negative disruptors around homelessness are toxic, making it difficult for solutions to gain traction. Pivot to a shared/common experience that reinforces the notion that people without shelter need the same things as everyone else: an address and the stability that it offers.

The Power of an Address

Washington, DC is one of the most prosperous and vibrant cities to live in the U.S. and home to many of the most powerful addresses in the world. Yet in the shadows of the White House, the Capitol buildings, national monuments, 175 embassies, luxury condominiums, upscale retail and restaurants, many of our neighbors do not have a home to call their own.

Having an address is powerful—whether you are a world leader, a business owner, or a childcare worker. An address is required to register to vote, to enroll your children in school, to get a government I.D. or to apply for a job, to file any kind of government claim, and so much more. Research tells us that an address, a place to call home, provides us with so much more than the actual house number conveys — a sense of belonging, a connection to community, the ability to plan for the future, better health & employment options.

While the region is home to a multitude of powerful addresses, far too many people in our region lack stable access to one. Often nestled between our high-profile addresses — the embassies, the monuments, the museums and the transit corridors — are tents that have become makeshift shelter to an increasing number of people who are locked out of the opportunity that an address provides.

Far too many of our neighbors lack the power of an address. They live in tents and sleeping bags in our parks and along our streets. Even more line up nightly to sleep in emergency shelters. Thousands more are living in unstable and often unsafe housing circumstances. Many of us know someone—a cousin, a friend, an employee—who is teetering on an edge so razor thin that any unforeseen event, expense, or challenge would put them in the street.

Despite the dire statistics about homelessness in our region, there is some good news to share. First, we are not alone. In fact, a small cadre of cities across the country are solving this issue by working together in multi-sector collaboration to redesign the systems that were meant to address the housing needs of their residents. It is our time now: time for our city to join a growing list of regions across the country that are tackling the issue of homelessness and winning.

In a region as prosperous as ours, with so many prominent leaders and some of the wealthiest addresses in the world — we can and must do better. This should not be our reality and it cannot become our new normal.

Our work will ensure that everyone who lives here, no matter the circumstance, has the power of an address.

Principle #3: Tell the Story of Us

Stories are so powerful. Research shows that in storytelling mode, we sit, listen, and think differently. Stories make information easier to understand and to digest. Studies have also shown that people recall information more easily when it is shared via stories than when people are given facts alone. Stories are also better at holding people's attention (because a good story gets people interested in how it unfolds).

Yet many of the stories that we are sharing to try to generate support for our work, leave out: (1) the stakeholders whose support we need, (2) those with lived experience of the issues we are trying to tackle, and (3) the systems that we are trying to change. As a result, we unwittingly leave people on their own to understand how they fit into the story and what THEIR responsibility is in solving the adaptive challenge we've outlined. Then, we leave them to guess how our call-to-action for system change has anything at all to do with their lives or our ability to solve this issue. So, our task is to harness the power of storytelling by including our stakeholders, our systems and those with lived experience in our stories.

We can tell all kinds of interesting, vivid and compelling stories as long as they are strategic — serving the goal to build broader public will around the case that we are making, by limiting the social distance around the issue.

3.Tell the Story of US

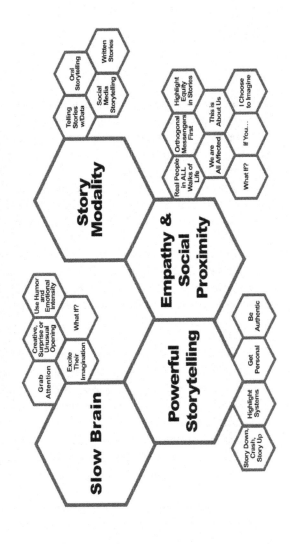

Reflection Questions:

- Are the stories that I am sharing about the problem and solution, centering those with lived experience?
- Am I also integrating the stories of a wide range of stakeholders and groups (many of whom may not have thought about how much they are affected by or implicated in this problem)?
- Am I widening the circle of people who see themselves as part of the problem and solution?

Your Ticket to Implementing This Principle

Storytelling allows us to engage and reach people differently. Stories give us the opportunity to be creative, to use humor, wit, vivid images, metaphors and to tap into people's empathy and emotion. So, take advantage of that opportunity. Tell the story of your work and who it benefits in entirely different ways; with faces and places that people would never have associated with your issue.

Sample Success Measures

- ☐ **KPI:** We are consistently telling stories that grab people differently, centering lived experience, systems and new stakeholders
- ☐ **Outcome:** Our stakeholders have more empathy for the people with lived experience; they see themselves and systems as part of the story
- ☐ **Impact:** New stakeholders are supporting our work; they have a stronger commitment and understanding of the work that we are doing; and they value people who have lived experience as integral parts of the conversation and solutions

WAKE UP PEOPLE!
Getting to the Slow Brain

Over the last 20 years, more people have become interested in psychologists' exploration of the two modes of thinking people use to process information. We might call them the fast and the slow brain (in deference to the acclaimed psychologist and Nobel prize winner Daniel Kahneman and his book, *Thinking Fast and Slow*).

The fast brain operates automatically and quickly, with little or no effort and no sense of voluntary control. This is the part of the brain that people use to respond to us when we approach them about supporting our work. This fast brain doesn't take us very seriously — it quickly dispatches with us, doesn't use much mental processing power to evaluate our claims, think through our solutions, nor think deeply about how to react to our call-to-action.

The slow brain, on the other hand, is the one we want. The slow brain is the part of the brain that allocates attention, allows us to focus and perform more complex mental functions. This slow brain is one that is more deliberative, and engages people's sense of agency, choice, and concentration. The slow brain allows people a chance to really think about what we're saying and to reconsider old/bad information they might have stored in their thinking.

Having people stuck in fast brain mode is problematic for us. So, our challenge (and opportunity) is to literally kick people out of the fast brain and into the slow brain. There are many ways to do this, but the easiest way is often to grab their attention in a creative or unexpected way, literally forcing them to stop and reconsider what you've said or presented. Using humor or unusual methods of engaging people can force them to stop, for just a moment, to really process what you are trying to do and to have them engage differently.

For example, a few years ago, there was the ice-bucket challenge that brought awareness to an important medical condition (ALS) and raised more than $115 million from all over the world. It was one of the most successful fundraising efforts in the history of nonprofit fundraising and it was successful not just because it raised money but because it "slow brained" people. It engaged them differently, in a relatively meaningless but fun activity, that went viral. It gave the nonprofit just enough time and space to open people up differently than if they had a formal fundraising appeal.

Similarly, the Nature Rx campaign uses an eye-catching and unusual way to remind people that many of the psychological "disorders" we suffer from today could be solved by...nature! That is, so many of the things that are ailing us are really about not having time for self-care and could be solved relatively inexpensively by having people spend more time outdoors, in green settings, mostly getting away from work or stress producing activities to enjoy the outdoors. Their online ads imitate pharmaceutical commercials in a funny and sarcastic way that engages people differently – kicking people into the slow brain for just enough time to have them stop and consider nature.

Another example, the Broccoli versus Kale campaign (The Broccoli Makeover) sponsored by the New York Times used a fictitious rivalry between two vegetables to expand public consumption of Broccoli. The ad team assigned to the campaign decided to "pick a fight with Kale" (a much cooler vegetable) in order to get more attention on this issue.

They created a fictitious Broccoli Commission of America, whose slogans include: "*Broccoli: Now 43 Percent Less Pretentious Than Kale*" and "*What Came First, Kale or the Bandwagon?*" and "*Eat Fad Free: Broccoli v. Kale.*" Picking on kale — rather than on, say, French fries — was especially brilliant because it mimicked the Great Soda War between Pepsi and Coca-Cola, an entirely bloodless battle that greatly enhanced the bottom lines of both companies.

Some of the local versions of the campaign created t-shirts, hats, buttons, other paraphernalia and sister ads to support the campaign. Most important, the ad campaign is said to have grown public consumption of broccoli by more than 102%. This wasn't just "creative marketing", it was about slow braining the content for consumers who were not likely to pay attention to a traditional conversation about the merits of broccoli.

If you are working on an issue that needs more attention, master the fine art of getting people to the slow brain — the place where they have to (and maybe they even WANT to) stop and figure out what you're talking about!

TRY ME! To bring public attention to the need to invest in beach restoration across the state, we worked with a statewide coalition to send postcards to legislators from the beach reminding them of how much our beaches are not only our playgrounds but bring in significant revenue for the state. Without attention to beach erosion, those things are in jeopardy. The post cards were one part of our campaign. We then had our advocates across the state put pictures on their social media pages from their vacations at various beaches across the state and tag legislators. The response was swift – we got legislators to pay attention and prioritize funds for beach restoration projects across the state. Here's a snapshot at what we sent and said.

Twenty Years Ago, We Were All Swimming at Our Beaches.
Now We're Swimming Upstream to Save Them.

Ten years ago, would have been a great time for a few strong, decisive steps to improve the quality, condition and care of our beaches. Ten years ago, the first state-wide beach erosion report was released, and scientists warned that without significant intervention to care for the natural environment of our beaches, that we could literally lose them. Ten years ago, none of this seemed as serious as it does today.

The world around us has changed quickly in the years since the first erosion report was released. The pollutants, the over-fishing and farming upstream, increased tourism and global warming, have all contributed to the need to adapt our response to caring for our beaches. Without strong, decisive, coordinated action across the state, the condition of our beaches will continue to erode, worsening the experience for our tourists, dragging down our quality of life, and limiting business and economic growth along our beachfronts.

But here's the good news. If the amount of time we spend on our beaches is any indication of how much we love our outdoors, our environment and our beaches, then our work to gather support to invest in them should be easy. With science on our side, unprecedented momentum from our state legislators and beach front coalitions actively engaging people across our state, we are now ready to take coordinated, decisive action.

Ten years ago, we were not ready but today offers us another, better pathway. Today, we act with strong, shared purpose on an issue that affects us all. The investment that we need to make in our environment is made from a recognition of our shared history, our strength, our adaptive leaders, and our desire to responsibly grow our state's economy.

The statewide initiative leading the charge on this issue was created to map the path to that better future, where we all continue to have access to the beautiful beaches we love, as well as to the restaurants and hotels that support tourism.

We'll do our work in this initiative by engaging voices throughout the state, and sharing expertise from all over, in this effort. We will put each unique beach community's preservation priorities front and center, while learning from the best of what other communities across the state are doing already. And we'll use that input to guide and measure our progress along the way.

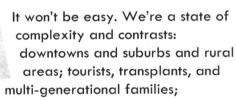

It won't be easy. We're a state of complexity and contrasts: downtowns and suburbs and rural areas; tourists, transplants, and multi-generational families; businesses and academia and government and nonprofits and faith communities; many cultural backgrounds, many languages, many different homes and circumstances, with different needs and uses for our beaches. No matter who they

THE story OF us

are or where they live in our state, they enjoy and depend on our beaches in some way. Now, we need something from all of them in return. We need everybody and all these voices engaged and pulling together — and dissenting sometimes too — to transform our shared future. We know what the consequences are of doing nothing, and it's not what we want for our environment or our beaches.

We need your postcards of love from our beaches, your stories, numbers, data, policies, dollars, expertise, capacity, organizations, and government agencies, of course. But most of all?

We need YOU. This is your home. The beaches are yours.

Welcome to the team. Get involved!

Principle #4: Anchor and Credential Solutions, Not Problems

So much of our messaging and engagement strategies have been crisis and problem oriented, that it proves difficult to have people WANT to engage in extended conversations/ relationships with us. We have become experts at explaining the problems we seek to solve and how they work, but we don't usually give the same attention to credentialing what would help. Also, the availability of more data (especially data about the problems in our neighborhoods and communities), has made it easier to tell crisis-oriented stories – credentialing them with a barrage of facts and figures. We typically leave the more inspiring conversation about solutions to the end and often, we even fail to offer up concrete statistics and data to anchor support for our call-to-action.

To make the case, our task is to engage people in the bigger aspirations that our solutions provide and to do that BEFORE we launch into a conversation about problems. When we anchor people in solutions (especially those that are future-oriented), we offer people the opportunity to be excited about the future that we can create together. We can invite them to think with us about how to bring that future into existence and we release them from being stuck in the quicksand of today's problems. Be clear though, this does not mean that we shouldn't talk about the problems and offer up sobering statistics, it just means that we do not START the conversation there.

4. Anchor & Credential the Solutions

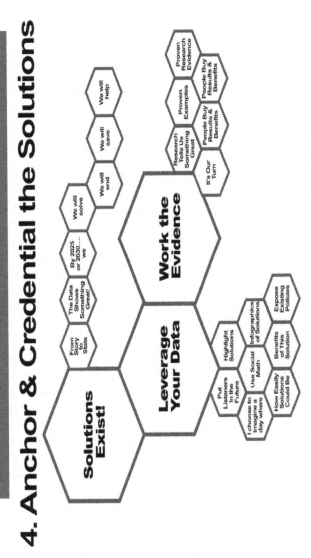

Solutions Exist!

Leverage Your Data

Work the Evidence

From Story to Stats

The Data Shows Something Great!

By 2025 or 2030..... we

We will solve

We will end

We will save

We will help

Research Tells Us Something Great

It's Our Turn

Proven Examples

Proven Research Evidence

People Buy Results & Benefits

People Buy Results & Benefits

Put Listeners In the Future

Highlight Solutions

Use Social Math

Infographics of Solutions

Benefits of This Solution

Expose Existing Policies

I choose to imagine a day where

How Easily Solutions Could Be

Reflection Questions:

- Did I anchor the conversation in solutions or simply default back to talking about the problems?
- Did I position the solutions as credible, achievable, forward-thinking, and feasible?
- Did I provide examples of where the solutions have worked in other places, to overcome cynicism and the negative disruptors (see Principle #2)?

Your Ticket to Implementing This Principle

There are two types of data. One type helps us to understand the magnitude and scope of the problems we need to solve; this type also helps us plan programs and investments. The other type of data inspires people to act because they are genuinely excited about their own future. The challenge is that we are often using the former, when we should be using the latter. Data-driven stories about how many people are poor, or hungry, or sick, or homeless (you name it), rarely gets people inspired. So, take the data you have and think about how you would present that information in a way that would inspire someone to lean forward or, collect new data that helps you tell a solutions-oriented story.

Sample Success Measures

- ☐ **KPI:** We are consistently using our data to tell solutions-oriented stories that inspire people about the future we can create together
- ☐ **Outcome:** Our stakeholders are using our data to talk more about solutions, then problems
- ☐ **Impact:** Our stakeholders are solutions focused; they are excited about the solutions we proposed, and they use our data to credential those solutions

---

MASTERING THE TECHNIQUES OF ANCHORING AND SOCIAL MATH

One of the most important and powerful casemaking strategies for leveraging data is a persuasive technique called **anchoring**. Attorneys, mediators, salespeople, and other skilled communicators often use this strategy to intentionally direct a conversation and enlist greater support for specific outcomes. Anchoring responds to the human tendency to give the most weight to the first piece of information or idea provided to us when making decisions. Given this cognitive bias, it is essential that, when making a case for change, we choose the first piece of information or data—as our anchor—strategically. The data you use literally "anchors" people's thinking, so our task is to use the data that invites and encourages a positive response to our call-to-action.

Over the last twenty years, the amount of data we have access to has literally exploded. If all I knew about you was from the data I could collect from your cell phone, laptop, online profiles, and your credit card statements, I could almost write your life story! At least, the outlines of your story anyway!

Yes, data is ubiquitous and the opportunity to use the data we're collecting about the state of our communities, our economy, our environment, our health, our homes, and much more, can be crucial in our casemaking.

Unfortunately, the way that most of us are using the data at our disposal doesn't often help our casemaking. We often start with negatively framed data that demoralizes people (reminding them of a whole lot of problems that seem too big to solve and totally out of their control), rather than exciting and engaging them in action. For example, how many of us working on health equity issues start our appeals for support with something like this — *"the leading cause of death in this county for young people aged 7 to 14 is _____"* or *"the growing rate of ____ in our state, is cause for deep concern."* Not very inspiring is it.

And for those of us looking to foster stronger support for addressing racial or economic disparities in health or who may be intentionally using a racial equity lens to make our case, we often start with a statement like this, *"...the rates for Black and Latinx populations are two times the rate for other groups — which is serious cause for alarm".*

I am surprised by how often I see advocates making a case for systems change by anchoring the conversation in the problems they hope to tackle. While the severity and urgency of the problems may have brought you and your partners to the table, talking about problems typically does not get people excited about joining an effort. In fact, a good body of research in the cognitive sciences consistently finds that our brains are wired for optimism—which means anchoring your case in problems makes it likely that your potential stakeholders will disengage.

Yes, this information is relevant and important, to be sure. It helps us to describe the shape and dimension of the problems we are trying to solve. We are able to point out where there are gaps to be closed, alarming trends to be aware of, and where our interventions might best be targeted. In every possible way, this data is critical as we work to develop innovative and impactful solutions that drive health improvements in our communities.

The challenge here is that leading with negatively framed stats like the examples above (as important as they are), is that they can make it harder to make the case. Negatively framed data may tell us more about the problem, but it also depresses our sense of engagement, agency and optimism about solving those problems.

More important perhaps, it tells me little about the possibilities for fixing those problems and does more to credential the problem, than the potential solutions. As a result, in most communities, people can tell you so much more about the problems they face than any of the feasible or recognized solutions to those problems. They rail about what's wrong, because they have great practice in reciting narratives about what's wrong, but they are often totally unaware of the solutions that already exist (sometimes in their own backyards) and need more support or scale. And so, when we probe about solutions, people they either give a blank stare or default back to their narratives of "individual responsibility" – displacing problems back on the very people who have not been well-served by our existing systems. While people should be exercising "individual responsibility", odds-defying resilience should never be our metric of success. We need systems to work better!

We know that data is important, but the point is that unless we are clear about its role in how we make our case, we will use it in a totally counter-productive way. That is, our sense that data is important for equitable systems change is not misguided – data matter – but the importance of using those data strategically to strengthen how people receive our calls-to-action, is what needs our intentional rethinking.

Let's get specific about some of the ways the anchoring technique can help us leverage our data and strengthen the case we are trying to make.

Use Your Data to Anchor Systems-Level Outcomes at the Top of Your Messaging, Saving Data About Individuals for Later in the Storytelling. Often, we use data to demonstrate the size, magnitude, and intensity of the problems we hope to solve. But, when we use data on the "front end" in this way, we essentially credential the problem and verify the need. So, instead, reinforce your case for systems-level change by using the data to anchor the systems-level solutions or approach that we are proposing.

If your goal is ultimately to change systems, you'll need to anchor people in systems level thinking right away. That means choosing a data point that reminds people of the systems we need to change. So, at the most basic level, anchoring a case for systems change means presenting systems-level solutions first and then consistently reinforcing and directing attention back to the need to change those systems. The more firmly you anchor data in systems-level solutions, the more likely it is that the resulting conversation among stakeholders will stay focused on systems change and that those stakeholders will actually have the conversation you need them to have.

> **Here's an example:** Many people in the affordable housing industry often make the case for change by highlighting how much individual renters or homeowners are paying for rent or mortgages. Because of their strong advocacy, an increasing number of Americans now understand that housing is a problem. That's the good news. The challenge is that most Americans have little understanding of the housing delivery system and what the constraints are for creating or preserving more affordable housing. So, the only level in which they can engage this conversation is at the level of consumption — i.e. housing as a consumer good. We know that this narrative of

housing as a consumer good is a huge backfire for the public discourse we want to have about changing housing SYSTEMS! So, if you want to change the conversation, we've got to change the way we use our data.

A better way to use data to highlight system-level outcomes is to highlight those constraints as opportunities for investment. A regional a housing survey of development and construction professionals in highlighted the constraints that are impeding their ability to produce more affordable housing. In the chart below, those constraints are shown as opportunities as identified by people working in the sector. More than anything else, our ability to improve the labor supply in this region would be a strong investment in their capacity, according to housing professionals.

Development • Construction Industry Member's Outlook

How Do We Ensure More Affordable Housing Gets Built?
Strong Investments in Housing Production Can Help

45% — Improving Regulatory Processes

76% — Improving Labor Supply

56% — Lowering Cost of Materials

By talking about the need for affordable housing in terms of the opportunities to improve the labor supply — it forces people to think about this issue at the systems level, in addition to the specific individual outcomes on people. We might follow up this chart with another showing how the investment in improving labor supply will help improve the cost of housing for renters and homeowners across the region. Focusing on labor supply might help us also position the issue of workforce development for the population of people likely to need affordable housing (that would be a 2-for-1, win-win).

Together, those data make a more effective case by anchoring people first in systems that need rethinking the (housing delivery system and workforce development system, for starters). It then allows us the space in talking about the resulting impact on the problem, to think through how those changes would transform the dynamic on the ground for renters and homeowners. But we wouldn't be able to get people there if we started this conversation talking about how much people pay for rent or for mortgages. We'd certainly get their attention, but ALL of that attention would then be focused on whether those renters and homeowners were "managing their finances" rather than on how we change systems so that they work better. If we want people to lean forward in a call-to-action that is about systems change, then a great way to use our data is to anchor people there right from the beginning!

Use Your Data to Anchor Systems Thinking by Creatively Helping People See the Systems That Are Usually Invisible to Them (Yet Those Systems Actually Determine the Outcomes They CAN See). Even people who work in your industry or sector may not always know how the eco-systems or inter-relationship of systems around our adaptive challenges work. That is, by definition, adaptive challenges usually involve multiple, intersecting systems that are woven together and interrelated in ways that few people really understand. In our last example the relationship between the housing delivery system and the workforce development system is a case in point. They are not things that average Americans tend to think about very much but the relationship between them determines in large measure, the cost and availability of the homes we live in.

So, we need people to better understand how systems work (or could be functioning differently, more efficiently and more equitably), else they can't fully lean forward in giving us the support we need from them. We discuss this issue in more detail in Principle #5 below, but it is worth the time to highlight how data can be used to help people see AND understand how systems function to produce the outcomes we see.

That is, a great use of your data is to creatively show people the systems that operate largely invisibly but actually determine the better part of the outcomes they can see.

> **Here's an example:** We'll stick with housing as an example here. Affordable housing is actually a great example because most people have no idea how affordable housing is created, built or preserved. The enormous work that it takes to finance affordable housing or to site it in neighborhoods (avoiding the not-in-my-backyard attitudes), the regulations placed on housing or the impact fees associated with such developments. And, the "to-do" list on affordable housing goes on and on, often discouraging developers who might be otherwise inclined to invest in affordable housing.
>
> Without understanding how layered and difficult it is to produce, site, maintain and preserve affordable housing, many people find it hard to answer our call-to-action. They don't understand why we don't just build more housing! So, a great way to use your data is to help them see what is largely invisible to them. Help them see the layered "to-do" list and understand how their support for systems change could help us do this adaptive work.

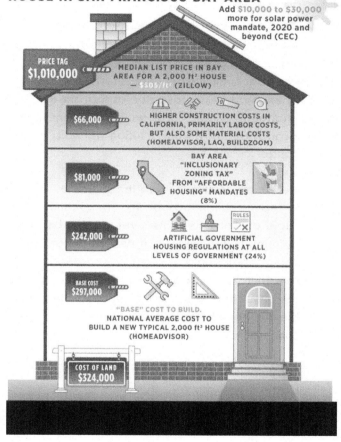

COST BREAKDOWN FOR A TYPICAL NEW HOUSE IN SAN FRANCISCO BAY AREA

Add $10,000 to $30,000 more for solar power mandate, 2020 and beyond (CEC)

PRICE TAG $1,010,000 — MEDIAN LIST PRICE IN BAY AREA FOR A 2,000 ft² HOUSE — $505/ft² (ZILLOW)

$66,000 — HIGHER CONSTRUCTION COSTS IN CALIFORNIA, PRIMARILY LABOR COSTS, BUT ALSO SOME MATERIAL COSTS (HOMEADVISOR, LAO, BUILDZOOM)

$81,000 — BAY AREA "INCLUSIONARY ZONING TAX" FROM "AFFORDABLE HOUSING" MANDATES (8%)

$242,000 — ARTIFICIAL GOVERNMENT HOUSING REGULATIONS AT ALL LEVELS OF GOVERNMENT (24%)

BASE COST $297,000 — "BASE" COST TO BUILD. NATIONAL AVERAGE COST TO BUILD A NEW TYPICAL 2,000 ft² HOUSE (HOMEADVISOR)

COST OF LAND $324,000

This example provides people with a way to breakdown the costs of affordable housing and to know where the levers of change in the existing systems are likely to be. Or simply, to at least understand why these costs exist.

Use Your Data to Anchor and Credential Concrete Solutions Within those Systems, Not Problems. Anchor your case in concrete examples where systems-change efforts have netted improvements in population health and/or reduced costs. This means being especially selective in providing examples and case studies that show systems change in action. Focus on the uniqueness of your approach and how your solution will help bring about change.

Here's an example: Health advocates working to reduce childhood obesity, for example, might anchor a systems-level solution by pointing to the number of new parks or open spaces that would need to be created or rehabilitated to provide children with an outlet for physical activity, rather than starting with the number of obese adolescents in a community.

They could share data on how the addition of just 20 parks across "green deserts" in a city, would likely reduce or "flatten the curve" on obesity rates in those

81% of U.S. teachers say kids' behavior changes positively after recess.

communities. They could also highlight what positive things happen for children, their families and the surrounding community when we flatten the childhood obesity curve. Having a fuller understanding of why and how solving this issue would help everybody (including these young people) is what helps people lean forward and get excited about the systems change work that you've asked of them.

Data on where there are "hot spots" of obesity developing across the region could be provided to share the rationale for locating parks in those areas of the city. And, the magnitude of the obesity challenge overall (the problem advocates want to solve) can be embedded later in the case, but by focusing attention on a systems-level solution first, the emphasis (and anchor) remains on the systems-level solution. Essentially, you have anchored people in thinking primarily and foremost about what would actually help. In this case, better parks and playgrounds for children.

Playrounds are designed to
PULL KIDS AWAY FROM THE SCREEN
and get them excited about outdoor playtime.

We think every child in every community deserves access to **FUN, STIMULATING PLAYGROUNDS.**

DURING PLAY, CHILDREN USE THEIR IMAGINATION
as they create fantasy worlds, act out different roles and express their emotions.

In addition, assessing data on how we can fight obesity through instituting system changes and influencing key stakeholders (like beverage manufacturers and restaurants to change) is extremely helpful. It reminds people of the systems issues that can help us tackle this issue at greater scale.

Be clear that this kind of us of data doesn't absolve parents, caregivers and others of taking responsibility for what children in their care eat, but it does anchor the solutions at a higher level so that there is balance in the conversations around this issue. If you don't anchor them in systems, the default to blaming parents for their children's obesity happens without any serious grappling with the broader issues that make it very difficult (even for very conscious parents and caregivers) to respond appropriately.

Use Your Data to Anchor and Inspire the Possibility of Change. Often the public imagination is limited in terms of thinking about how we might actually solve some of the problems we face. To help expand their sense of possibility and optimism about the prospects for change, use your data to give examples of how we might solve the problem — even out-of-the-box examples help. Give examples of how we've solved similar issues like this one in the past or how other industries, organizations, agencies, or residents, were able to triumph in solving similar problems. These examples help to overcome people's cynicism about what is possible and help get them committed to solving the issues that challenge us.

> **Here's an example:** The Institute of Medicine (IOM) of the National Academies made a set of recommendations to address critical inefficiencies across the health care system. Here they highlight the inefficiencies in the use of data and information. The IOM could have simply highlighted the costly inefficiencies in the health care delivery system because we are not using data and information effectively but instead, they chose to highlight how the same kind of information (even sensitive information) is shared in other industries. Their point was to highlight the possibilities for change in the health care system and to inspire action. In the example below, they highlight the solutions and then share how those changes could help overcome health care inefficiencies.

USE INFORMATION TECHNOLOGY MORE EFFECTIVELY

Clinicians and patients should have real-time access to medical records and use technology to streamline administrative tasks.

IN OTHER INDUSTRIES...　　**IN HEALTH CARE...**

ACCOUNT HISTORY

ONLINE BANKING

allows customers to view their entire financial history and conduct transactions in seconds.

50%

Almost 50% of patients report that information necessary to their care was not available when needed.

25%

of patients said their health care provider has had to re-order tests to have accurate information for diagnosis.

Here's another of their examples.

IMPROVE TRANSPARENCY

Patients and clinicians should have easy access to the prices of tests and procedures and to reliable information about care outcomes and quality.

IN OTHER INDUSTRIES...　　**IN HEALTH CARE...**

Before shopping for an

APPLIANCE

or booking a hotel, consumers can compare prices and look at reviews of performance.

85%

PLAN A AN B

of people had not been informed by comparative quality information about their health care.

2/3

of patients feel that as long as it is so hard to find the price of care, controlling costs will be difficult.

*Use Your Data to Create "Social Math" that
Helps You Anchor and Inspire the Possibility of
Change.* **Social math** when used effectively can help
you relate the data you have about the solutions you
propose, to other meaningful visual cues that people
already relate to. Mastering the fine art of relating
your solutions to things that people already relate to,
is a great way to translate your data effectively for
casemaking.

So, relating homelessness to holiday decorations
(something most people have some experience with),
helps them to connect to the solutions you propose.
That example is below.

> **Here's an example:** Health advocates working
> to reduce solutions to homelessness might share
> data-based examples of how we might pay
> for the cost of shelters, housing and services for
> homelessness in this country and provide homes
> for all by, redirecting all of the money that we
> spend on holiday decorations (see the
> diagram shared in this Huffington post story).
> By comparing the costs of these interventions to
> something most people take for granted, it
> excites their sense of what is possible and
> makes the large problem seem conquerable.

> Be clear — our point here is not to really ask
> people to stop purchasing their holiday
> decorations. To the contrary, our point is to
> make people reconsider what is possible and

give them the space to ask questions about the possibility of other solutions.

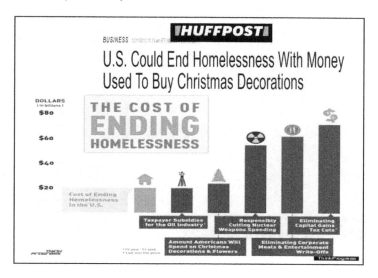

Social math for casemaking can be effectively created in a variety of ways. The approach above (homelessness intervention related to holiday decorations) is the first approach. It means taking the data you have and comparing it (in scale and number) to something that is more easily understandable to your stakeholders.

Here's another social math example: We could also highlight the possibilities of what we could do by switching to solar power. By laying out the possibilities, we excite people's imagination of what could be done and give them a way to think about the possibilities for solving this issue.

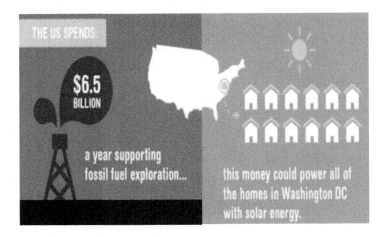

Here's another example: The alcohol industry spends more than $2 billion every year to advertise and promote consumption by college students. This amounts to approximately $225,000 every hour of every day.

The result? Enough alcohol was consumed by college students last year to fill 30,000 Olympic-size swimming pools. The overall amount spent on alcohol per student exceeded the dollars spent on books and was far greater than the combined amount of all fellowships and scholarships provided to students.

So, we can ask ourselves if our societal investment in alcohol is a useful one and how we might help our young people make more lasting investments in their (and our) future. Then, we might highlight the broader social and economic consequences of these investments.

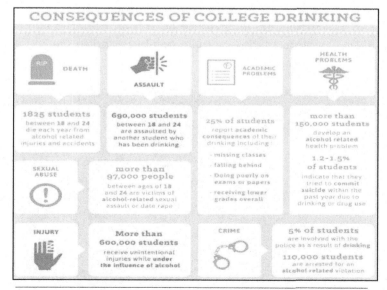

Another variation uses social math to break numbers down, making the problem smaller and more easily solved. This is important because some of the most profound social issues feel too big to be solved. We can use our data to bring the problem down to a level that people can start to imagine how it might be solved. Let's continue with the alcohol consumption example.

> **Here's an example:** One of the most common ways of using social math to highlight the impact of an issue but break it down into smaller numbers so that people can absorb its importance is to look at time and money. What's the incidence of the issue over a period of time (in the example below, in minutes) and how much does it cost ALL OF US in dollars (in the example below, an annual amount). Again, the importance here is that people can relate to these smaller numbers and to the concern with costs.

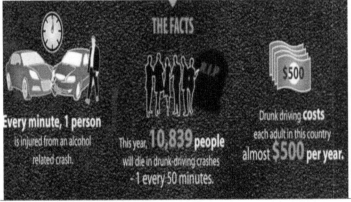

THE FACTS

Every minute, 1 person is injured from an alcohol related crash.

This year, 10,839 people will die in drunk-driving crashes - 1 every 50 minutes.

$500

Drunk driving costs each adult in this country almost $500 per year.

Here's another example of social math but applied to the issue of prescription drug use. Here, the larger number of painkillers is reduced to the day, per capita. By doing so the advocates make this something most people are likely to be able to digest and understand.

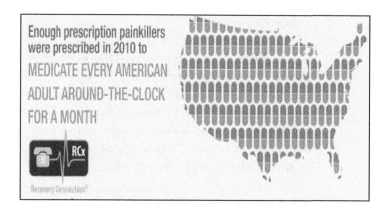

Use Your Data to Anchor People's Thinking on the Logic of the Different Policy Approaches and to Help Them Arrive at the Conclusion that Our Existing Policy Arrangements Are Not Serving Us Well. Yet another way to use data in this regard is to highlight how our existing policy choices are not logically consistent and may not be serving us well in terms of the impacts they engender.

Here's an example: Because policy is made at all levels of government and in different agencies, it is not uncommon to see one branch of government or agency promoting an outcome that another branch or agency is discouraging. Highlighting this disconnect is a good use of our data, because it helps people come to the conclusion that we need to change course — choosing a thoughtful and consistent policy direction.

Our example here comes from the education space. Head Start (something we are currently defunding at a rapid pace) has actually been shown to have a larger effect on children's early achievement than homework (for older children). If Head Start is working to great effect, why defund it?

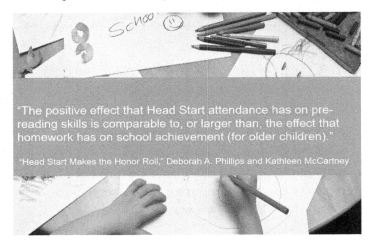

"The positive effect that Head Start attendance has on pre-reading skills is comparable to, or larger than, the effect that homework has on school achievement (for older children)."

"Head Start Makes the Honor Roll," Deborah A. Phillips and Kathleen McCartney

Similarly, here is another example highlighting children's exposure to violent media. The relationship between violent media (video games, television programing, etc.) and aggression (especially in children) is larger than many of the things we currently regulate. So why have we not focused more squarely on regulating or at least addressing violent media as well?

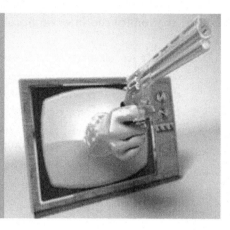

"The correlation between violent media and aggression is larger than the effect that wearing a condom has on decreasing the risk of HIV,...larger than the correlation between exposure to lead and decreased IQ levels in kids,...larger than the effects of exposure to asbestos, larger than the effect of secondhand smoke on cancer."

Brad Bushman,
Professor of Psychology, Iowa State University

Use Your Data to Anchor People's Thinking in the Benefits of Our Collective Intervention at the Program, Policy or Investment Level. It goes without saying that the primary reason that we are using data as part of our casemaking is that we want to bring awareness to issues and then elevate the need for some kind of intervention. It's interesting however that most of us use our data to credential the problem but not to credential the interventions. In other words, we actually need more information and data on the intervention than we do on the problem itself. Most people who see your data and who will listen to the case that you are making are likely to have some familiarity with the problem and its magnitude/dynamics. But they may know very little about the intervention you propose (how it works, who it would help most, limitations or drawbacks, as well as the benefits that would accrue to everybody because you are intervening in this way). So, use your data to credential the intervention.

> **Here's an example:** If we continue with the alcohol consumption example, we could gather data on how a wide variety of community actors, institutions, agencies, or residents could directly intervene. Here's an example that focuses on health care providers and it's a great use of data anchoring. Anchoring people in the kind of intervention that might be most helpful.

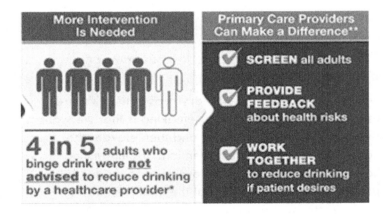

More Intervention Is Needed

4 in 5 adults who binge drink were **not advised** to reduce drinking by a healthcare provider*

Primary Care Providers Can Make a Difference**

✅ **SCREEN** all adults

✅ **PROVIDE FEEDBACK** about health risks

✅ **WORK TOGETHER** to reduce drinking if patient desires

Here's another recent example many of us have seen with the COV-19 virus. This simple graph, shared thousands of times, helped ordinary Americans start to understand the severity of the issue and importance of the proposed 'social distancing' intervention.

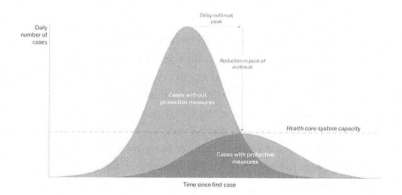

Use Your Data to Anchor People's Thinking in the Connections Between Issues that Are Critical to Solving Adaptive Challenges (Especially on Connections That They Don't Have Much Practice Thinking About). Adaptive challenges are unique in that they are issues that know no boundaries — that is, they are typically interrelated problems that require more holistic resolutions. Yet, many of us are not practiced in thinking holistically about the challenges we are seeing in our communities nor with tackling those challenges as holistic issues, so the approaches we implement are often siloed.

Data can help us move people to more holistic, cross-sector alignment, if we understand its power to drive the conversation in those directions. Whenever possible, use your data to highlight the connections between sectors, issue-areas or communities to anchor people's ability to think more holistically about the issues at the heart of your case.

> **Here's an example:** Often the challenges that people and communities face show up in the doctor's office. That is, many physical ailments are the result of broader social determinants that physicians and medical professionals are not equipped to addressed but they deeply impact our health. The same is true of schools, where teachers see the impacts of children's homelives in the classroom, but they are not often empowered with the resources to address those issues impacting their students' achievement.
>
> Here is an example of how to use our data to link health and wellbeing to broader social determinants in people's imagination. The data here speaks to the fact that many physicians would love to write prescriptions for the broader social issues that are making their patients sick — lack of affordable housing, jobs, nutritional assistance, healthy food programs, etc. but they do not have the ability to write those prescriptions. Physicians

overwhelmingly believe that this would improve patient care and outcomes. And, 3 out of 4 physicians surveyed said they wished health insurers would pay for additional costs associated with connecting their patients with relevant services, since it would take them additional time and money to assess these additional needs and make referrals or recommendations to community partners.

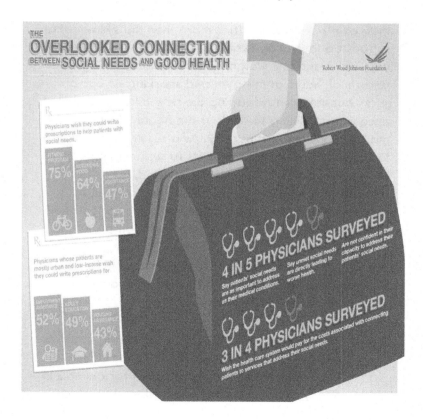

Use Your Data to Anchor a Future Orientation.
Additionally, leveraging data for public will building
means anchoring the conversation in the future! The
future is something we can create together and
intentionally. So, one of the most important things you
can do to build support for your systems-change effort
is ensure that it has a strong future orientation at the
front end.

People tend to romanticize past successes, recalling
their own personal sacrifice more than the systems that
supported them. For example, someone who worked
very hard and lost weight might look back years later
and recall hours at the gym and snacking on carrot
sticks but not acknowledging the new bike lanes that
encouraged biking to work or the healthy food
markets that opened nearby. As a result, when people
look backward, their willingness to support systems-
change efforts often decreases. Instead, invite
stakeholders to imagine the future they can help
create and use your data to reinforce that orientation.
We'll present a more fulsome conversation about the
technique of "future pacing" in Principle #7, but here
we share some examples of how data can help you
shift your audience into the future orientation that
strengthens your case for change.

> **Here's an example:** Our example here comes
> from the animal shelter field. Often relegated
> to providing care and protection for animals in
> need, one such shelter decided to set a much
> higher and fundamental intention. By 2030

their goal is to end animal abandonment in San Francisco.

Another example of using data to enhance a future orientation is to underscore the impact that you expect in the future due to the investment that you are asking your stakeholders and strategic partners to provide. That helps them to see the outcomes that you are after (and expect to have), as well as to keep the conversation forward facing. Here's one that shares what an animal shelter might try to convey.

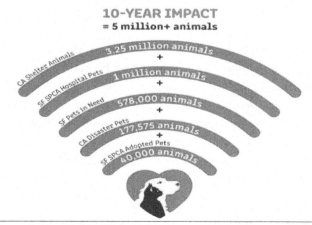

And here's another example on homelessness. The idea here is to anchor public thinking in prevention and what it will take to flatten the incidence of homelessness in this community.

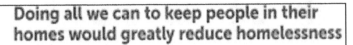

Doing all we can to keep people in their homes would greatly reduce homelessness

By 2026, maximizing prevention would bring homelessness down by 27%

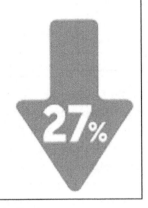

27%

This kind of use of data is especially important on issues like homelessness where public spending in some communities has increased to solve this issue but unfortunately, despite the best efforts of housing advocates, the data shows that the problem has grown significantly in recent years. The future focus here is meant to help overcome the likelihood that this data on homelessness will become a negative disruptor — reminding people of how helpless they feel about solving this issue. As we discussed in Principle #2, if you do not reframe this conversation, the data will be used as a negative disruptor and will actually backfire because it will limit people's sense that something good can come from our intentional work to intervene.

Use Your Data to Anchor the ROI (Return on Investments) On Your Issue and Position Them Side-by-Side with the SROI (Social Return on Investment). One of the absolute best uses of our data for casemaking is to give more specificity to our conversation about the investment we need to make in our future. When we talk about the future and its possibility, people can certainly get excited but when we pair that proposition with concrete numbers on the return-on-investment (ROI) and the social return on investment (SROI), we are able to give even more credibility to our solutions. Moreover, when we use established research or evidence-based practice alongside our SROI data, we solidify our rhetorical claims with greater clarity and increase the "odds of success" to our stakeholders.

> **Here's an example:** The data used to support housing programs, services and investments is often lodged at the current direct benefits to people. But most of these interventions have benefits that go far beyond their direct beneficiaries and beyond housing. Here is an example of a housing organization being explicit about how the investment in housing actually translates in other residual (but equally important) benefits.

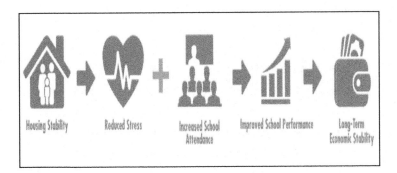

Housing Stability → Reduced Stress + Increased School Attendance → Improved School Performance → Long-Term Economic Stability

Below is another example focused on health care that shows the adaptive challenge, how employers can lean in to improve employee health, and what the return on their investments have been shown to be in research and clinical evidence.

Use Your Data to Anchor People's Thinking About the Societal Allocation of Resources on Your Issue and How Those Resources Might be Differently Allocated. For many casemakers, the issue of how resources are spent — either by government or by corporate entities — is a major issue. Resource allocation is an important role that governments often control or regulate but it can be difficult to get people to focus on that issue. Data highlighting misaligned resource allocations (intentionally or those misalignments out of natural consumption patterns) are important.

Using your data to highlight how resources are allocated AND THE IMPACTS OF THOSE MISALLOCATIONS, can be a great way to leverage your data in the service of public will building. Use that data to prompt a series of questions about how we could re-align those allocations (or regulate them when they show up as part of natural consumption) to better effect. Our earlier example of college students' consumption of alcohol and how it outstrips the money they spend on books and tuition, is one example. See others below.

> **Here's an example:** A look at how our resources for wellness are spent in the United States shows allocations that many would be surprised to hear and would prompt a conversation about how to shift these dollars. In the United States we spend substantially

more (2x) on personal beauty aids (likely a result of the billions in beauty marketing by corporate retailers), as we do on preventative and public health. Yes, we all want to look our best deep into our elder years (and hence, the focus on anti-aging aids) but when we put those numbers side-by-side, most people would say that their preference would be to shift those resources to public health and preventative care — especially in light of the recent COV-19 outbreak.

Let's state here again, it may not be possible to shift beauty and anti-aging cremes (something the beauty industry would likely fight anyway) but making that comparison opens up the possibility for thinking more expansively about how we spend our resources and what kind of resource re-allocations ARE feasible.

Here is an example that highlights how lobbying has a huge ROI but likely has opportunity costs for other kinds of investments that could be served by these funds.

Use Your Data to Anchor a Redirect or Pivot the Conversation Back to Your Narrative. In Principle #2, we focused on the art of an effective pivot. The data you choose and how you wield that data can help you make an effective pivot away from issues that are not helpful and back to the narrative that builds support for your case. During the process of a pivot, data can be used effectively to redirect the conversation back to the anchors that are more meaningful and constructive.

Here's an example:

The start of the conversation about health care:

"Americans have choices, and they've got to make a choice. So rather than getting that new iPhone that they just love and want to go spend hundreds of dollars on that, maybe they should invest in their own health care. They've got to make those decisions themselves."

-- Rep. Jason Chaffetz during a CNN interview. March 7, 2017

<u>The pivot back</u> to the narrative the health care advocates want to have about health care costs.

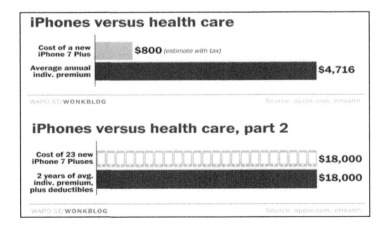

What's important to note here (as stated in the discussion of an effective pivot in Principle #2), is that this is NOT about refuting the argument directly. Sharing this data simply allows you the space to pivot back to a narrative that is more helpful. So, you might say something like, *"Yes, I'd love to talk about the cost of iPhones. I even have one myself. A brand-new iPhone or some other variety might cost someone $800. But that's not nearly what a health care premium costs workers in almost ANY occupation in the United States. So, let's talk about what health care premiums cost workers and who can afford to pay that. The data I share below puts those costs in better perspective. And if you'd like, we could even call each other on our iPhones to talk about that!"*

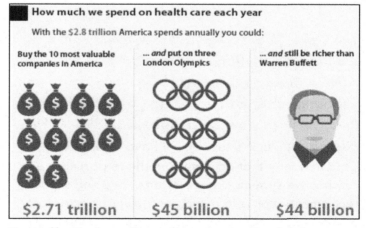

That effectively redirects the conversation back to data that helps you to have the conversation YOU want to have and that is more meaningful to the issue at hand.

$16,655
Average annual premium per
enrolled employee for a family
on employer-based health
insurance.

$5,832
Average single annual premium
per enrolled employee for
employer-based health
insurance.

Less than $1,200
It's estimated 8 in 10 individuals can choose a Marketplace plan with a
premium of *$100 or less per month* after tax credits.

*The Only Time It is Helpful to Anchor Your Case
with Negatively Framed Data is When You Have
A New Piece of Data that is Startling or
Shocking. Use that One Data Point and Then
Pivot Back to How Solving the Issue Would Help
Everybody.* In this section, we have focused on using
data in a way that activates people to participate in
constructive systems change efforts. In doing so, our
recommendation is to avoid negatively framed data
at the top of your casemaking. It doesn't mean you
cannot use such data, it just means DON'T LEAD with
that negative data. There will be opportunities as you
work to right-size your interventions and solutions to

revisit the data that speaks to the magnitude and dynamics of the problems you are working to solve.

There is however one circumstance where leading with negatively framed data can be to your advantage. If you have one dramatic data point that is new — meaning, it is not something most people familiar with the issue know about. Using that data in your case can be helpful because it "slow brains" the issue. That is, it opens the case with something unusual that can grab people's attention in a new way.

<u>Here's the caveat, you only need ONE data point negatively framed</u> and then pivot quickly back to your solutions. In other words, use the data as the flash point in the conversation but quickly get back to stronger ground — how do we tackle this issue.

> **Here's an example:** In most of the world, children cannot be sentenced to death or life-sentences in jails. The United States is one of the few places in the world where this is the case. Highlighting how rare it is that we engage in this practice and the impacts on their families, can be a game-changer. Keep in mind too that in this example, we highlight a system practice that is ripe for our advocacy and system change efforts.

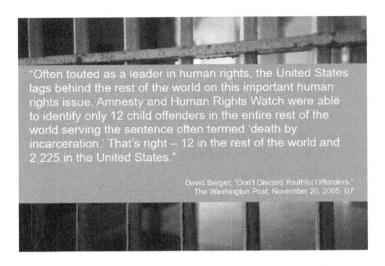

"Often touted as a leader in human rights, the United States lags behind the rest of the world on this important human rights issue. Amnesty and Human Rights Watch were able to identify only 12 child offenders in the entire rest of the world serving the sentence often termed 'death by incarceration.' That's right – 12 in the rest of the world and 2,225 in the United States."

David Berger, "Don't Discard Youthful Offenders," The Washington Post, November 20, 2005, B7

A Final Word: Be Careful Not to Use Labels in Your Data that Stigmatize Certain Groups or Use Data in Ways that Can Lead to "Othering". Negatively framed data is problematic for many reasons, one of the most important is that you can inadvertently contribute to stigmatization or reinforcing stereotypes or bias. Rethink how you label the groups in your charts – labels like "at-risk" or "homeless people" or "under-privileged" – all stand the risk of reinforcing very unproductive negative biases and stigma. You can make the same points with your data to distinguish groups without negatively labeling people. Actually, think about what would happen if you labeled people in terms of their potential for greatness, rather than their vulnerabilities?

Here's an example: Many organizations working with people who are experiencing homelessness, simply label them as "homeless people". But homelessness is not a characteristic of innate abilities, it is a condition or experience that people are facing. So, let's call it what it actually is. This example takes a statistic that is normally presented in the negative case and with the negative label (i.e. the number of "homeless people" who die every day). Here, we show this in a different way — how many people experiencing homelessness could be saved because of the investment our community is making in this issue?

Through the Investment We Are Making in Our Community, We Will Save the

36 people who are experiencing homelessness

and die EVERYDAY

To Avoid "Othering", When Possible and Appropriate, Use Your Data to Present the Universality of Problems, Even When Your Policy Solutions Target Specific Groups or Sub-Populations (i.e. Often for the Benefit of Equity Concerns). It is very easy for people who are experiencing poverty or other challenging circumstances to be labeled or "othered" because of our data. One way to avoid that is to demonstrate the universality of the problem (where appropriate) and then let your narrative speak to the reasons why you have chosen to focus on particular groups or populations.

> **Here's an example:** Almost all Americans are experiencing increases in their housing costs relative to their budgets. Yet, most housing organizations single out low-income families and talk a lot about the fact that many of them are "housing cost burdened" — meaning, they pay more than 30% of their income for housing. By framing it this way, they can easily be "othered" by people who will say "those people" simply lack the ability to manage their finances properly.
>
> While it may be true that people can manage their budgets better (couldn't we all?), that is not the primary reason so many Americans are struggling to afford a decent place to live. Instead of talking solely about the plight of

people who earn low wages, show the universality of what is happening and THEN, explain the rationale for focusing policy on those groups.

Here is an example showing that people at all income levels were paying more of their income for housing in 2014 (the blue bars) versus 2005 (the red bars). So, this is an experience that is happening to EVERYONE, not simply to people earning low-wages.

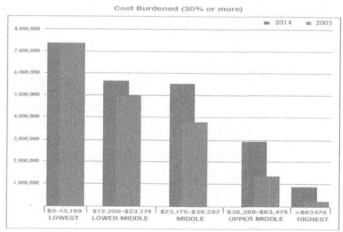

Cost Burdened (30% or more)

This kind of representation makes it difficult to suggest that workers with low wages are somehow less capable of managing their finances than others. We might however argue (as many housing advocates do) that people earning lower wages may have to make tougher tradeoffs to pay rent than others and so, our focus on those workers is warranted.

Another example uses social math and the full income distribution to help people understand why this moment is important and why we need an equity lens. While this group could have given a traditional chart, saying something like this: The bottom 20% of US family incomes grew by only 6% between 1979 and 2008. This is a major decline when compared to income growth between 1947 and 1979. They didn't!

Instead, they highlight how all groups (except the top income earners) are faring different outcomes than they did in previous generations. By showing the full spectrum, it makes it more difficult to "other" low-wage earners to suggest that they are doing something uniquely WRONG!

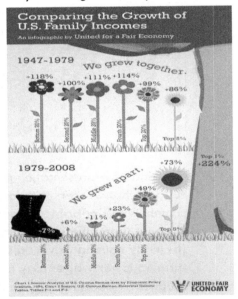

nother example below shares state-wide data on the incidence of poverty. This graph shows that no matter where you live in the state, there are children whose family incomes are so low that they live deeply in poverty. In other words, this is not a Miami problem or an Orlando or Tallahassee problem. This is an adaptive challenge that is state-wide. The magnitude in each county might be different but the challenge itself is spread across the entire state. This representation makes it difficult for people to create unconstructive narratives othering or stereotyping different parts of the state.

There are 944,415 children under 18 years old living in poverty in Florida. Here is where they live.

Source: 2015 Data from U.S. Census, American Community Survey

Anchoring and social math are important pro-tips. The opportunities for creative, accurate use of data are considerable, and the value of these pro-tips are great. As you use them, just be sure that your data, stats and comparisons are accurate and defensible.

 INSTEAD OF THIS: After more than a decade of progress in improving high school graduation rates, there remain about 1,300 traditional high schools in need of serious improvement and redesign, according to new research from the GraduateNet campaign. Among them are more than 800 low-graduation-rate high schools with an average graduation rate of 49 percent. From the inner city to the heartland, these high schools sit at the fault lines of race, class and inequity in the US.

 TRY THIS: We are winning the battle to improve high School graduation rates — we've already improved learning and graduation rates at 4,500 schools nationwide. Now, let's finish what we started — working to improve and redesign the remaining 1,300 schools with low graduation rates. We will redouble our efforts to provide resources, expertise, counselors and student assistance to the 800 high schools with the lowest graduation rates. And, by 2030, our efforts will ensure that every high school across this nation, no matter where it is located, prepares its students for success and sends them out with an earned degree! By investing in the students who need it most, we will address the equity issues at the center of our educational system and better academic achevement for all students. Will you join our effort?

 INSTEAD OF THIS: There are 4,475 children in foster care in our state. It's important to pause in our hectic schedules to remember these statistics:

- 1 child becomes homeless every 14 min
- 1 child drops out of school every 60 min
- 1 child is abused/neglected every 60 min

We know that some of the children in these statistics are OUR CHILDREN. They attend our schools, live in our neighborhoods, maybe even have dinner at our tables. They are the reason we do so much to focus on PREVENTION.

 TRY THIS: Our future depends on our ability to ensure that the 2+ million children in our state have the resources, resilience, and strong start in life that they need to carry us forward. This is an awesome responsibility to steward the future of so many children in our state. We've done a lot already to help the children across this state have what they need to thrive and are on the road to success in our great state.

Our work now is to make sure that the 4,475 children who remain in foster care across our state, get the same great start. Have we done enough to ensure that these children have the bright future that we all envision for all our children? We know that with a focus on prevention — helping families avoid foster care entirely and ensuring that the 4,475 children already in foster care across our state, find stable homes.

Here's why it matters! With our help, some of these children will become nurses — working the front lines in our hospitals or caring for our growing senior population allowing many of them to age-in-place. Some will become business owners, lead some of our most innovative companies or serve in public office. Some will become police officers — helping to maintain law and order in our communities. Some will be managers of the retail outlets where we shop — helping us to choose ripe produce or select that perfect suit for our daughter's wedding. Some will become teachers and social workers — helping us to prepare the next generation of children for success.

Our success is riding on our ability to pull ALL of our children forward. No one wins if so many of our children do not have what they need to thrive. No one wins if so many children experience long-term homelessness, that they never learn how to function in stable families into adulthood. No one wins if children across our state have so little to start with, that they become more susceptible to child predators or drug dealers.

We only win, when our children, all of our children, have what they need to survive: stable homes, adults who surround them in love, and communities who nurture their success.

4,475 brilliant lives are in our hands – join the effort to ensure their light continues to shine in every communty across our state. Let's make sure that the challenges they've already faced leading up to their placement in foster care, only gets better from there. Let's make sure that the future ahead of them, looks better than their pasts. Help us to fight as hard for their futures, as we fight for our own children.

You can join us by:
- **Advocating** on behalf of fostering in our state
- **Contributing** your time and expertise to our foster parents as resources
- **Sponsoring** a "foster day" at your place of worship, school or place of employment
- **Fundraising** to help us close the gap in funding that our agencies get from public dollars.

Principle #5: Make the System and Equity Issues Visible

Often, I hear leaders talk about the need for "systems change" and equity. They recognize that the systems most of our communities depend on were designed long ago and are not functioning well to address the wide range and scale of the adaptive challenges we face today. Moreover, those systems too often reflect old values and social norms that don't result in equitable outcomes.

Even so, building support for systems change and for equity can be tough, especially when most Americans do not understand how those systems were designed in the first place; how they can be redesigned to be more equitable; and they are unclear about how changing those systems would actually improve their lives.

As a result, leaders seeking support for systems change that would produce more equitable outcomes, have to work hard to make those systems visible — explaining both what those systems do, why they are essential to everyday people's lives, and how they can be redesigned to function better for everybody.

Because this can be A LOT of information to add to your case, this is a place where the use of an explanatory metaphor helps make a complicated system much easier to understand.

Metaphors related to systems change typically sound like this, our system functions like a "vaccine", helping to protect families from negative outcomes or like a "smart car" helping our residents navigate the tough challenges they face in finding adequate health care or housing options. And, even the words "systems change" can function as its own kind of metaphor, especially when we use it to stand in for the world we want to shape.

Given that the adaptive challenges we face as a nation will require us to vastly shift how our systems operate, means that we will need to master the ability to help people understand what that actually means with as little jargon, technical language, or formal definition as possible. If our work is to make the case to technical audiences, they will already know something about the systems we are working to improve. But because most of our casemaking will likely happen in front of people who lack that expertise and are unlikely to listen to long-winded explanations, let's get busy wielding the powerful sword of metaphor!

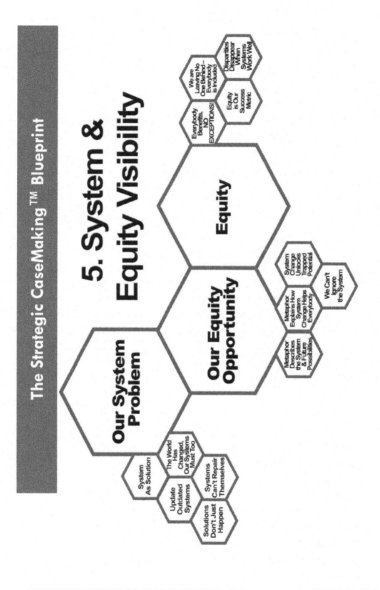

The Strategic CaseMaking™ Blueprint

5. System & Equity Visibility

Our System Problem

- System As Solution
- The World Has Changed, Our Systems Must Too
- Update Outdated Systems
- Systems Can't Repair Themselves
- Solutions Don't Just Happen

Our Equity Opportunity

- Metaphor Describes the System & Future Possibilities
- Metaphor Explains How System Change Helps Everybody
- System Change Unlocks Trapped Potential
- We Can't Ignore the System

Equity

- Everybody Benefits, NO EXCEPTIONS!
- We are Leaving No One Behind – Everybody is Included
- Equity is Our Success Metric
- Disparities Disappear When Systems Work Well

Reflection Questions:

- Am I making the systems that I want to change visible in my conversations with stakeholders?
- Did I talk about what those systems do, how they function (and malfunction) by using an explanatory metaphor?
- Did I give specific examples of how changes in those systems will have practical benefits for people?

Your Ticket to Implementing This Principle

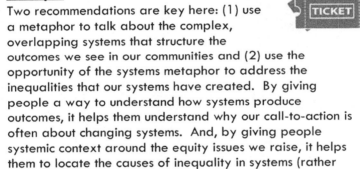

Two recommendations are key here: (1) use a metaphor to talk about the complex, overlapping systems that structure the outcomes we see in our communities and (2) use the opportunity of the systems metaphor to address the inequalities that our systems have created. By giving people a way to understand how systems produce outcomes, it helps them understand why our call-to-action is often about changing systems. And, by giving people systemic context around the equity issues we raise, it helps them to locate the causes of inequality in systems (rather than the failings of the people we are trying to help).

Sample Success Measures

- **KPI:** We are consistently directing the "action" toward systems by using a powerful metaphor that helps us explain inequality
- **Outcome:** Our stakeholders are using our metaphor to describe the intervention we need to take together and describe equity issues in the context of relevant systems
- **Impact:** Our stakeholders are systems and equity focused; they understand that the "action" is in system change

USING METAPHORICAL THINKING TO MAKE SYSTEMS VISIBLE AND EMBED AN EQUITY LENS CONSTRUCTIVELY

Metaphors can be a powerful and important part of your casemaking. Generally, metaphors are powerful shortcuts that help people to understand complex structures like our health care system or our workforce development system, without the long-winded explanation experts usually offer. Because of this, metaphors can do the heavy lifting as you engage people about the systems change you hope to inspire, as well as help you build support for equity as part of your system change work.

So, what's a metaphor and how do we use it our work? Ever heard someone say, "Time is money." That's a metaphor. How often have you heard that statement? Probably many times and in various contexts. By thinking about time as money, you can create a powerful mental image that helps you (or others) reprioritize time. For many of us, we'd like to help people "reprioritize" how they view our work to reform the systems around us — especially those systems that are woefully out-of-date and those that exacerbate problems or reinforce existing inequities.

What about these related metaphors?
- **Time wasted is money down the drain.** (*emphasizes efficiency and the need to avoid waste*)

- **Time well spent is an investment.** (*emphasizes seeing time as a value, wanting to maximize that value, and the desire to see dividends or benefits from it*)
- **The seconds are ticking away.** (*emphasizes the urgency of the moment and how we measure that urgency — literally in increments of seconds*)

Each of these metaphors is working toward helping people reprioritize their time but each grabs a slightly different metaphor that reinforces a different aspect of time. This is important because the metaphor that you choose to use in your work should help you to convey the kind of system change work that you are trying to do.

At their core, metaphors are really just fancy ways of comparing two unrelated or indirectly linked things. The visual mental picture that we get when a metaphor is used though, helps us boil down concepts to their most basic elements and engage in rapid sensemaking. The metaphors we use in casemaking work by associating an unfamiliar idea with one that is commonplace, so that you can spark better understanding of complex ideas.

Here are a few ways that metaphors can be helpful in your systems change work and some general metaphor examples to spark your creativity in making your case. Also, because we know that equity issues are best expressed as part of the systems metaphors, we offer some examples here on that as well.

Use a Metaphor to Break People Out of Their Fast Brains and Get Them into the <u>Slow Brain</u>!

Often it is helpful to relate two things that seemingly have nothing to do with each other to break people out of their old ways of thinking about an issue. By breaking the rules of logic in this way, metaphors can open the creative, deliberative side of the brain – the part that is stimulated by images, ideas, brainstorming and concepts. In this way, metaphorical thinking can help you "slow brain" the conversation and help people connect to their brainstorming and problem-solving power. To use another common metaphor, I'd say that metaphors help us "*think outside the box*".

If you are using the metaphor to open up people's creative energy for thinking through solutions, don't get too hung up on how well the metaphor maps back. Metaphors that map too well can stifle the creativity you are trying to generate! The whole idea is to generate ideas, solutions and reflections that you may not have otherwise thought of, so just let the ideas flow without too much scrutiny if your goal is ideation.

I use this technique in community meetings when I want them to think bigger about the possibilities for investment and development of their communities / neighborhood. When I want them to be expansive in generating ideas, a good set of metaphors flies.

I will often offer up a bunch of metaphors on a white board and start by asking people to pick out the ones that most closely describe how their neighborhood or community operates today and then, ask them to pick a second one that best describes how _they'd like_ it to operate. Then, I ask them to try to see if they can come up with their own metaphors to describe their neighborhood and when they do, we start to try those metaphors on together.

Here are some examples:

Our community operates like a:

- a garden where it nurtures the people who live and work here

- a checkout line at the grocery store that moves very slowly, where we have plenty of time to talk to one another, but very little actual community-building gets done

- factory where everybody has a job to do but they focus solely on that job and don't really see the whole community or have a holistic view of it

- an expensive jewelry store where the shopkeepers follow you around, and you do not feel welcome or like you ever really belong here

- like a playground, where people are free to explore new things, connect constructively with neighbors and share community resources

Use a Metaphor to Explain Complex Systems, How They Work When They Function Well and How They Fail When We Are Not Vigilant About Updating or Repairing Them. Start here by using the metaphor to describe what the system is intended to do and then talk about why it has failed to live into that intention.

Here's an Example: *Our education functions like a conveyor belt. It is supposed to move our students from elementary school through high school and then into careers. When it works well, the conveyor belt pushes people along at appropriate intervals as they achieve higher levels of proficiency. About 10 years ago, it started to sputter, graduating so few students from one grade level to the next, that it negatively affected our entire community. Few students were getting what they needed to move along, and they did not have the wherewithal to adjust. So today, our conveyor belt has come to a full stop, especially for the children who most need formal resources to achieve. Few students graduate and those that do, find themselves so unprepared for the available jobs that they quickly give up finding one. We need to rethink how our educational system prepares our children for success and make changes that adapt schools for the outcomes we need from them. We need a new conveyor belt – one that is built for the world we live in today. One that*

has the tools to prepare our children for success
and that moves them from one level to the next,
as they achieve proficiency.

Use a Metaphor When You Want to Identify Workable Solutions to System Problems. The
solution ideas you have generated for the
metaphorical problem can help your stakeholders find
a workable solution to the real problem. By first
talking about how systems are currently designed and
secondarily how they are ill-designed to address the
issues facing our communities today (in some way), we
provide them with a mental framework to work from.
Then we can ask about the kinds of solutions that might
solve the metaphorical problem and ask, how might
that apply to our real-world problem.

Here's an example: In the previous example
about schools, we might ask them to talk about
what a conveyor belt does and how it
operates? What gives that mechanism power
and what happens when it breaks down? How
does it get fixed, who maintains it and how do
we know when we need to replace it? Once
they've answered those questions, then we ask
them to apply what they know about conveyor
belts to the real-world problem of graduation
rates.

Here's another example: Racial segregation
is a de facto rule in most communities across
our nation. So much of how we invest in

communities is still shaped by old, outdated bigoted practices that the time has come to rethink community investment. A well-functioning community investment system would not produce this much segregation, instead it would operate like a well-functioning regional transit system.

Transit systems provide open and shared access to the major roadways, central arteries and pathways across the region in a way that is more efficient than other more individualized modes of transportation. They connect people to local modes of transit and also to broader national modes of transportation (like Amtrak stations or airports). A well-functioning community investment system would offer the same kind of universal access, maximize efficiency and connect communities to broader national investors or funding streams.

When a community investment system is working well, the system is visible to everyone (like transit maps); the system effectively fills gaps or mitigates those hard-to-reach places so that all communities have access to capital investments (like transit extenders or first/last mile options); and there are some players in the system who are "super-connectors" that ensure stability and efficiency (like transit stops that connect multiple transit lines together or weave together multiple modes of transport in multiple directions).

In the same way that most regions have come to understand the importance of creating an infrastructure to support transit, many are starting to understand the importance of organizing a well-functioning community investment system.

As our policymakers look to make high-return investments in our future, the work we do to build the infrastructure in our community investment system is critical.

We simply cannot adapt to the promising future in front of us if we continue to drag old issues like racial segregation with us. We need an infrastructure that allows us to adapt and move forward in an inclusive and equitable way. We need an infrastructure that opens up new access to capital to invest in all communities across our region. That's how we change the imbalance of resources across communities, that's how we begin to address racial segregation, and that's how we ensure the pathway to opportunity. Join us as we build the cross-sector, cross-community partnerships to build the community investment infrastructure in our region.

Metaphors are Also Helpful When You Want to Talk about Disparities Across Groups, Equity or Fairness but You Do Not Want to Reinforce Negative Stereotypes or to Engage in "Othering". When we lift up disparities across groups — like health disparities between people of color and whites or inequities in social outcomes like homeownership, if we are not careful to talk about those disparities in the context of the systems that created those disparities, we risk people making default assumptions about the groups we want to help. In particular, we risk provoking those dominant narratives about "individual responsibility" or the narrative of "racial difference", in a conversation where we want systems change to be centered.

No one doubts the incredible power of average, everyday people to overcome amazing and fantastic odds but people should never have to demonstrate odds-defying resilience to survive. We need systems to work better. So, when we use a systems metaphor and then talk about who has access to those systems, we spark a more constructive conversation. Let a strong metaphor help you do this heavy lifting.

> **Here's an example:** Our housing system has evolved over time through a century of incremental changes. Some of these arose from policy decisions, others from the evolution of custom and practice. Evolutionary change can work well. But sometimes we see such profound

changes to our environment that we need a deeper and more thought-out response in order to overcome a systemic problem. This is one of those times.

Our housing delivery system today operates like a five-gear manual transmission automobile. When the car works well, we have homes being built at all income levels (or at every gear): 1st gear serves people with very little income (often folks who are susceptible to homelessness); 2nd gear serves low-to moderate-income rental markets; 3rd gear serves high-end rental markets and 1st time homebuyers; 4th gear serves high-end real estate markets; and 5th gear serves commercial real estate needs.

Today however, our housing delivery system is not functioning well. In most regions of the country, our car is stuck in 3rd and 4th gears — producing very little housing beyond these two groups. A car operating in only two gears is not only incredibly inefficient (allowing safe travel on only a few roads) but is actually quite dangerous to everyone — the driver, the passengers, the pedestrians and the other cars on the road. That's what has happened to housing in our country. Any mechanic would pull this car off the road for fear that it would endanger the wellbeing of many people. We need our policymakers to do the same. Pull this car (or our housing system) off the road for repair.

We need a housing system that doesn't put us all in jeopardy but rather, one that helps us all get stably housed. We need decisive action to redesign the housing delivery system so that it functions efficiently, works better for everyone, and produces diverse housing options for people at all income levels. Anything less puts us all in danger.

We need all five gears fully functional and operating. Because the first two gears are where the highest needs are, the initial work to improve the housing delivery system should start there – creating housing opportunities for people with very little income (but who still deserve a decent place to live) and those who are low-to-moderate-income renters.

These groups struggle the most to find affordable places to live because our housing system caters to those in higher income brackets. Historically, we have not served these two groups well – racial and income discrimination, redlining, restrictive covenants and other system barriers have made it more difficult for the gears to work effectively, producing fewer options there. Thus, we need to redefine success so that we understand that our system is operating effectively when people in first and second gears have as much access to housing, as people in any other group. In other words, only a housing system that ensures access to people in the lower end of the income spectrum can claim to be working optimally.

This is urgent and important work. Help us as we rethink how we provide housing resources across the country, as we modify policies, increase investment, and focus immediate housing assistance on the millions of families not being well-served today.

Take the time to read through the detailed plan on our website, offer your support for this work, and help us intentionally plan for a housing system that gets our car "in gear", operating at peak performance for everybody.

Use Your System Metaphors to Convey the Need to Grow, Scale or Better Deliver a Solutions that is Working. Metaphors are great mechanisms for helping to convey how and why your solution works best as well as for communicating the need to grow the reach and scale of that solution. So, if the case that you are making is about the need to elevate a solution or to advance the need to invest in and scale something that is already working, a metaphor might help you do that.

> **Here's an example:** Women are critical to the advancement of all communities, but women's contributions are especially important in nations that experience high levels of poverty. In the 1920s, the Ghanaian scholar James Emman Aggrey said, *"If you educate a man you simply educate an individual, but if you educate a woman, you educate a whole nation."* A World Bank study found that every year of secondary school education is correlated with an 18 percent increase in a girl's future earning power. And research shows that educating girls has a multiplier effect. Better-educated women tend to be healthier, participate more in the formal labor market, earn more, give birth to fewer children, marry at a later age, and provide better health care and education to their children. Investing in women is like **a ripple effect** — it not only helps the woman involved but it also prospers the entire community.

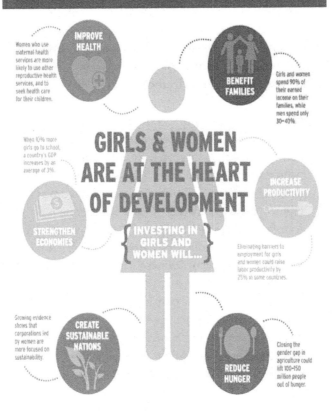

INVEST IN GIRLS AND WOMEN: THE RIPPLE EFFECT

IMPROVE HEALTH

Women who use maternal health services are more likely to use other reproductive health services, and to seek health care for their children.

BENEFIT FAMILIES

Girls and women spend 90% of their earned income on their families, while men spend only 30–40%.

When 10% more girls go to school, a country's GDP increases by an average of 3%.

GIRLS & WOMEN ARE AT THE HEART OF DEVELOPMENT

INVESTING IN GIRLS AND WOMEN WILL...

INCREASE PRODUCTIVITY

STRENGTHEN ECONOMIES

Eliminating barriers to employment for girls and women could raise labor productivity by 25% in some countries.

Growing evidence shows that corporations led by women are more focused on sustainability.

CREATE SUSTAINABLE NATIONS

REDUCE HUNGER

Closing the gender gap in agriculture could lift 100–150 million people out of hunger.

WOMEN DELIVER

WHO WINS? **EVERYBODY.**

Use Your System Metaphors to Help People Understand the Value of Your Organization, Coalition, Agency or Group to Leading the System Change Effort. As part of your work to underscore how systems function (and malfunction), how they can be improved and the work to redesigned them, take the time to share how your team fits into the work. We talk more explicitly about sharing your value proposition in Principle #9 later in this Guide but you can get started by positioning your team as part of the system metaphor that you create.

> **Here's an example:** Our coalition operates like a flywheel (or simply a wheel built on an axis that stores energy that can be redistributed). Flywheels preserve momentum so well that the energy stakeholders add to spin it faster in one part of the system, adds more to the capacity of the whole system. We are working to ensure that the energy we spend gathering and feeding insights from our community health practitioners back into the system, helps us to target and resolve the biggest points of friction across our health system. Together we are the flywheel that ensures better service delivery in our system and improved health outcomes for everybody.

There is no "right metaphor" — the ideas can be as unrelated as you like. But there are some general tips for making sure that your use of metaphor works well in the case that you are making.

1. *Make sure your metaphors are understandable and instantly ring true with your audience.* If people cannot understand the relationship between the two things you are relating, it won't help you very much. So, calibrate the metaphor to the group to which you are making your case.

2. *Be clear about what it is about the system that you want to change* and use the metaphor to describe that. Are you working to change its delivery or financing model? Perhaps you are working to better connect community resident or industry consumers to the solutions? Perhaps you are working to operationalize equity by embedding a racial equity lens or health impact lens or another kind of lens, into the decision-making process?

   Whatever the goal of your system change effort, the metaphor you choose should help you highlight that kind of change. Once you are clear about what about the system you are trying to change (i.e. where change is needed to improve and grow more equitable outcomes), then you can work on metaphors that help you to say that simply.

3. *Think of other instances in life where that same characteristic, idea, emotion, state, etc. applies.* You may be trying to get your stakeholders to understand the you are accelerating the pace of innovation (*maybe a race car or rocket ship metaphor*); you may be helping to connect those stakeholders to valuable resources (*maybe wiring, telephone or Wi-Fi are metaphors that help you*); perhaps, you are describing the kind of collaborative spirit you are working to develop with your strategic partners (*sports team, orchestra or other team building metaphors*). Identify the kind of change that you are working toward and choose metaphors that tell that story.

4. *There may be many metaphors for the situation you are describing – choose the one that will best relate to your audience.* Once you've done some creative work to think about what system change you are trying to create, test a couple of them to ensure they work well with the people you are talking to. Informally, you can test them with your stakeholders to gauge their reactions directly or you can hire formal researchers to test a series of related metaphors to see which work best for the groups you are trying to engage.

⟡ TRY ME!   Over the last 20 years, community developers have worked hard to advance more equitable development and healthy communities. Yet without stronger investment in our infrastructure (our ability to meet the changing environment around us), our power to impact the lives of those who need us most, is limited. As we watch economic inequality rise, climate disasters happen repeatedly, housing affordability move out of reach of average Americans, the stakes are higher, and the journey to opportunity is more difficult. When these emergent challenges are coupled with the long-standing structural and institutional barriers that have curtailed opportunity, especially within communities of color, we are made even more aware of just how critical investment is in community development. Shouldering the historic legacies of racism and bigotry that have stripped households and communities of wealth does not have to continue to be the path of our nation. This is unjust and our investment in burrowing a different pathway should be one of our nation's highest priorities.

The good news is that we have more knowledge, information and opportunities to help. That's why our work to provide our version of **the smart car** for a field that is still driving ineffective back office functions, needs stronger support. Our service specifically addresses some of the toughest challenges we face as a nation by strengthening the capacity of community developers and bringing new resources to communities that have historically faced disinvestment.

Like a smart car, we work to advance the navigation systems of our field. We provide strategic guidance that helps seasoned community leaders do what they do best (drive programs and services to assist residents) but with the benefit of assistance in key areas like human resources, accounting, and other back office functions. As independent non-profits, each member remains in the driver seat setting its own destination; we assist with navigation providing high-level program expertise and leadership. Under the hood, our back-end administrative services ensure that its members see the road ahead clearly, remain focused on what's ahead in their lanes and can travel as efficiently as possible. When our drivers (partner CDCs) have the freedom to focus on their mission, strategies, and impact, their journey is easier, and their work is more impactful.

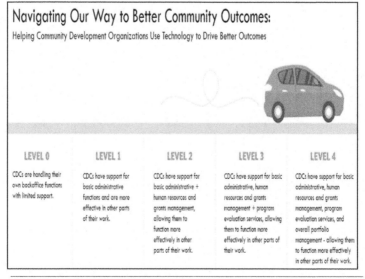

Navigating Our Way to Better Community Outcomes:

Helping Community Development Organizations Use Technology to Drive Better Outcomes

LEVEL 0	LEVEL 1	LEVEL 2	LEVEL 3	LEVEL 4
CDCs are handling their own backoffice functions with limited support.	CDCs have support for basic administrative functions and are more effective in other parts of their work.	CDCs have support for basic administrative + human resources and grants management, allowing them to function more effectively in other parts of their work.	CDCs have support for basic administrative, human resources and grants management + program evaluation services, allowing them to function more effectively in other parts of their work.	CDCs have support for basic administrative, human resources and grants management, program evaluation services, and overall portfolio management - allowing them to function more effectively in other parts of their work.

Principle #6: Shared and Collective Responsibility

One of the most powerful dominant narratives in our country is *individual responsibility*. How often have you heard your neighbors, friends or colleagues say something like "those people need to take personal responsibility for what's happening to them"? While it might be true — often people do need to build their own sense of agency to solve the problems they face — society also bears some responsibility for making tough decisions that WE have forced them to have to make. This is especially true when we think about large scale problems that are not likely to be resolved by individual level behavioral changes. Because the systems around us shape so many of the outcomes we see playing out in communities, it is even more imperative that we attribute some of the responsibility to our community.

Our task in generating a stronger sense of collective or shared community responsibility is to frame these issues as broader community level challenges in the first place. This is our opportunity to help community stakeholders think about how they benefit from solving the issues we raise. In particular, the more we help people see themselves as implicated in creating the challenges we are trying to solve, as well as in the resolution, the more they see their stake in working with us toward the resolution. Most people will not lean forward unless and until, they are made to see their stake in it. That's the work of Principle #6.

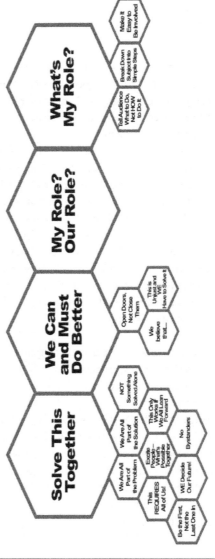

The Strategic CaseMaking™ Blueprint

6. Shared Stake/Collective Attribution of Responsibility

What's My Role?
- Tell Audience What to Do, Not HOW to Do It
- Break Down Subject Into Simple Steps
- Make it Easy to Be Involved

My Role? Our Role?

We Can and Must Do Better
- Open Doors, Not Close Them
- This is Unjust and We Have to Solve It
- We believe that...

Solve This Together
- NOT Something Solved Alone
- We Are All Part of the Solution
- This Only Works If We All Lean Forward
- We Are All Part of the Problem
- Excite People—What's Possible Together
- No Bystanders
- This REQUIRES All of Us!
- WE Decide Our Future!
- Be the First, Not the Last One In

Reflection Questions:

🐞 Did I make it clear that this is an issue that is OUR responsibility to solve?

🐞 Did I position our responsibility as an investment in OUR future rather than as charity to other people?

🐞 Did I make it clear by using concrete examples that we all benefit from solving this issue as a community concern?

Your Ticket to Implementing This Principle

Whether we like it or not, one of the strongest motivators for action is self-interest. The key to opening up a bigger sense of stake in these issues is to help people see their self-interest in advancing the collective. That helps people see, that when other's in the community win, so do they. Use your data to help them see the dividends (social and economic) that they get from the investments made in people they may never know and in communities where they may never live.

Sample Success Measures

☐ **KPI:** We are consistently reinforcing through our messaging and with our data, that we ALL benefit from the investment in people and communities

☐ **Outcome:** Our stakeholders are describing this issue as OUR responsibility to solve and about the benefits WE reap from solving it

☐ **Impact:** Our stakeholders see the resolution of this issue as inextricably connected to their own social and economic wellbeing

CROWDING OUT THE NEGATIVE TALK ABOUT GOVERNMENT AND ACTIVATE THE BYSTANDERS

Let's tackle the challenge that stumps even the best and well-resourced efforts to advance system change in the United States today – the role of government! This issue is as old as they come – our country was founded by people challenging the role for government, so it stands to reason that even today, if you are going to activate people to change the world around them, you have to position the role of government very carefully and effectively. What is the best role for government? How big or small should government be and what are the consequences of changing government's role in ensuring a standard of living for all Americans?

Over the last 30 years, in particular, our notion of "government" has taken a beating in the public imagination. From former President Reagan's harmful and consistent definition of government as "the problem itself", to his skillful wielding of the "welfare queen" caricature, cemented negative public assessment of government for many people in our nation. Reagan's painting of government programs as wasteful and spending on the "undeserving" was so successful that it continues to disrupt conversation about what government can and should be able to do.

But to be fair, it would be wrong to assume that it was only Reagan beating this drum - similar narratives exist on both the progressive left and conservative right that demonize our government for exacerbating a host of problems that continue to plague our nation. And, many of those assessments (like the role our government has played in creating racially segregated housing and neighborhoods) cannot be denied. They are true.

Luckily our task in this volume is not to resolve how people perceive government. You likely have enough already on your plate and do not need the additional lift of having to fundamentally change how we see government. Yet, if we are to be effective in making a case for change, we will have to grapple with how to effectively position government in our narrative. So here's the deal.

Today, there is such an enormous about of cynicism about solving the scale of the larger adaptive challenges we face (like poverty, affordable housing, health care, education, etc.) and people's support often gets hung up in their negative assessments of government. That is, people generally assign the bigger challenges to "government" to solve and when our government institutions cannot single-handedly solve these challenges, the failure reinforces the default perception that government is to blame and cannot be a constructive agent of change.

This is really a shame because while our government may in fact have its issues, we also have to acknowledge that we have not always given our governmental leaders the "best hand" (or the best tools and resources) for it alone to solve any of the adaptive challenges we face. That is, the solutions we need require the alignment of all sectors and a great number of institutional partners and stakeholders. Getting that level of cooperation and stakeholder alignment is tough. But more important, it literally means that not much is possible around issues of equity unless more of us are leaning forward.

The casemakig challenge for those of us working to solve truly adaptive problems, is that government is a necessary and important partner. Yet, for many Americans, "government as an agent of positive change", is a nonstarter. This is important because so much of the public opposition we hear related to contemporary public policy proposals, fall short under the weight of this now fairly common belief that government is part of problem and cannot be part of the solution.

This presumption means that our government (which most people see as outside of themselves), simply cannot be made to ever operate in the best interests of average, everyday citizens. The fact that our current political system (which people associate with government) is in full meltdown, with so much polarization and in-fighting, reinforces this all-too-common perception.

This creates a dangerous dynamic where we rail against government, become bystanders in our own lives, and then ask people to support our efforts to embrace government (through policymakers) to create better outcomes! Or alternatively, we do not ask much of our government or our leaders because we assume their incompetence and inability to solve problems, that are clearly too large for us working alone to shoulder. Let's face it — most of us feel overwhelmed by all of the so-called crises that seem to be happening simultaneously around us and it's just easier to deposit all of that stuff at the feet of government leaders and then complain because they (alone) cannot fix it.

To overcome this bystander mindset, we have to be very strategic in how we make our case. Otherwise, it is easier for people to relegate problems to government and then complain when governmental leaders cannot deliver.

There are a number of ways to activate bystanders in how we make the case. Chief among them is that we'll have to master the fine art of crowding out government in our stories by telling bigger "stories of us" (that is, stories of shared responsibility, obligation and sacrifice for the broader whole). Telling stories of shared responsibility, where we divide responsibility for solving adaptive challenges across a wide array of community leaders and institutions, reinforces a bigger message about the value of each.

This can take a number of directions.

(1) Start the call-to-action by explicitly saying, *The only way this issue will be resolved is if you and I make it happen. There is no calvary coming to save us. There is no one group or organization, no agency or messiah coming with all the reinforcements we need. There are no quick and easy solutions. This is hard work and we will all need to roll up our sleeves to contribute to this solution.*

(2) Then, call for the question by saying something like, *So here's what the banks are doing to help. Here's what the hospitals are starting to do to help. Here's what the YMCA is doing to help. Here's what the community organizations are doing to help. Here's what I'm doing to help. What will you contribute to help?*

(3) Then, reinforce the value of their unique contribution by saying something like this, *I'm glad you can help in this way. We literally would not be able to solve this without you. Are there others in your social network — your friends, family, co-workers, neighbors, kids teachers or coaches, that you could help us to engage and get them involved? We need as much help and support as we can get?*

(4) Then, bring government back in! *And, we will make progress so much faster if we ask corporate, governmental, nonprofit and*

*community leaders to lean forward as well. We
all have a unique role to play. We need
corprate leaders to do even more by...we need
governmental leaders (at all levels) to do more
by...we need nonprofits to do more by...we
need community leaders to do more by.....
Systems only change when we are all working
together to make change happen and when we
are united in our direction.*

Most people (although not all) will offer to contribute
in some way, once they know that others in their same
community have contributed something. What often
stops people from leaning forward is when they feel
like there isn't a real shared sacrifice.

So our task is to position shared sacrifice first in our
conversations (no matter how small those initial
sacrifices of others may be) and then to ask for
people's contribution as well. Once we've been able
to get them out of bystander mode and mindset
(because they can see the sacrifices others are
already making), then together we can advocate for
better governmental policies. The latter, of course, is
the bigger ask.

The strategy here is to crowd out the negative talk
about government that happens when the case that
we are making allows people to displace the
problems on government. Some of those problems
may be exacerbated by government but they cannot
and will not be solved WITHOUT government. So,

positioning government as merely one actor in a much larger set of actors is key, if our goal is to get people to take action, responsibility and agency for the adaptive challenges we face.

This casemaking principle is likely to be one of the toughest in practice because we have become so accustomed to villainizing government, that to have a message that seese government as a partner, alongside other partners (like corporate leaders) will be difficult for some. But if you don't position these leaders as partners, not only do you ensure that you won't get their partnership but you won't be able to move broader public audiences to action. They'll stay stuck in villainizing others (government and corporate leaders alike).

Also be clear, this strategy does not mean that you cannot have a healthy critique of government leaders. But it means that if your goal is to inspire people to "get off the fence and pitch in to help", a long, ongoing negative diatribe about government is unlikely to help. It will instead have the opposite effect. In an environment where people are so polarized and distrustful already, having you pile more critique on, only serves to undermine the eventual deals that you'll need to broker with those governmental leaders, if you are to be successful.

Instead, if you have a critique of government, state it clearly and unequivocally, then follow it up directly with a series of reasons why you believe this moment is a unique opportunity to partner more effectively than ever, with a whole range of leaders including governmental leaders, agencies and institutions.

This rule holds true as well with other types of leaders whose partnership is necessary for your work. If a strong critique is necessary, state it explicitly then, follow it directly with what gives you optimism that the partnership you need in those leaders can and will emerge. If you're not able to get there — to a place where you have a positive way to shape the partnership you'll need with those leaders you want to critique, it is unlikely that you will get other people (those bystanders) to lean forward to support your work. Think of it in this way — with all of the fighting and calamitous tension in the world to day, who wants to be join into a cat fight with you?

Our City, Our Future: Together, We Will Decide Our Future

Over the last twenty years, we've made extraordinary progress in revitalizing neighborhoods across our city. And here's the thing: none of it was inevitable or could have happened without the extraordinary collaboration we have experienced. We have worked across sectors, creating stronger partnerships than ever before. We have needed every business, every resident, every nonprofit, every city agency and our national partners working with us, to do this well. It was the result of tough choices we made together, and the result of your hard work and resilience.

Now, the task to keep us moving forward is one that falls to all of us, as well. Sustaining and building on all we've achieved — from having mortgage lenders develop customized programs for families in targeted areas, to developers hiring more young people in the building trades as they create more affordable housing, to our corporate partners helping us to invest in shovel-ready projects, to our city agencies protecting our drinking water and storm-water management, to our nonprofits contributing new playgrounds for our kids — that's going to take all of us continuing to work together.

Because that's always been our story — the story of ordinary people, conscious employers, caring nonprofits, civic organizations and our city government coming together in the hard, slow, sometimes frustrating, but always vital work of self-governing.

Here's what we have learn for sure. Having dilapidated neighborhoods in a city as prosperous and innovative as we are, just doesn't make sense. We decided long ago that poverty and blight are too expensive for us. The loss of human potential, the hopelessness of those living in crime-ridden neighborhoods and the health consequences – all come at a price much too high for us to pay.

Why allow poverty and blight to be facts of life for so many in our city when we have the power to prevent and perhaps even, eliminate them altogether? What if it were possible to break up the cycles of poverty and community disinvestment? That's the journey we are on and we are not waiting for someone to develop the "app" to fix this, we are doing it ourselves. Together!

People from all walks of life, in organizations and businesses all over this city are putting in the hard work to find new ways to work together, to plan together and create new ideas for revitalizing our neighborhoods.

Are there some things that we could do better? Yes, we have a long "to-do" list, to be sure. But we will not wait for "perfect", when so much "good" can come now. We will not miss the opportunity to invest our time, money and resources in improving the systems that determine how our neighborhoods grow and function.

Today, we stand on the shoulders of decades of authentic community development from hundreds of people across this city, holding a steadfast commitment to racial justice, climate resilience, and shared prosperity. Through collaboration with local and national nonprofits, banks, corporate and civic leaders, we are shifting the model of how our city invests in people and our neighborhoods over the long-term.

"There is no power for change greater than a community discovering what it cares about."

Margaret J. Wheatley

Principle #7: Creating a Catalytic Moment by Connecting to What's on the Strategic Horizon

Your stakeholders are not living in an isolated bubble. They are responding to a wide variety of adaptive challenges, issues, concerns and opportunities both in the present but also some that are likely to occur in the future. You are more likely to get their attention when you connect the issue you are trying to solve with a bigger catalytic moment or an issue that is marked URGENT for your stakeholders! For example, a new transit system is being built in the region which could open doors for creating affordable housing or co-locating other community resources. A natural disaster may have recently happened (think COV-19, wildfires, floods, hurricanes), prompting new resources to be delivered around community building and it may offer up the opportunity to think about resilience.

Whatever is on the horizon, your ability to *"hitch your wagon"* to it, typically makes it easier for you to garner the attention and visibility you need with stakeholders. The good news is that there are plenty of big challenges facing your stakeholders that are likely very relevant to the case you are trying to make. Go ahead and identify the bigger catalytic moment on the horizon and draw the dotted line for your stakeholders, between their urgent moment (or one that is looming) and yours!

7. Strategic Horizon & The Catalytic Moment

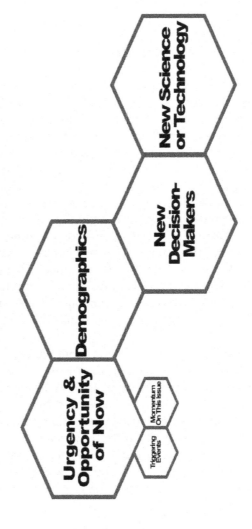

Reflection Questions:

- Do I have a clear understanding of what big opportunities, fears or challenges my stakeholders are facing?
- What are the big adaptive challenges facing my stakeholders?
- Did I connect my issue with a trend, an event, an investment or some other catalytic moment that my stakeholders are concerned with?
- Did I use my data or vivid stories to connect my issue with that catalytic moment?
- Did I provide examples of how a collaboration with my stakeholders would help connect to something on their strategic horizon?

Your Ticket to Implementing This Principle

Start by thinking through the pain points that are relevant for your stakeholders. What are THEY trying to solve for and how does your solution actually help them to do so. Think carefully about who (besides you and your organization) NEEDS to solve your issue (whether they know it or not) and help them to see how helping you, actually helps them solve issues that are relevant and compelling for them.

Sample Success Measures

- ☐ **KPI:** We are explicitly and consistently tying our issues to those that are already important to our stakeholders?
- ☐ **Outcome:** Our stakeholders start to talk about this issue as if it solves a problem or pain point that THEY have.
- ☐ **Impact:** Our stakeholders see solving the adaptive challenge as inextricably connected to their ability to solve THEIR problems (both present and future)

FUTURE PACING:
GETTING TO THE HEART OF THE
FUTURE WE FACE TOGETHER

This is one of my favorite casemaking techniques —
mostly because it is one of the easiest to master.
The idea of future pacing is simple. When you give
your stakeholders and strategic partners a window to
the future, you put them in a stronger disposition to
say yes to your call-to-action. Generally, people can
be very cynical when you ask them to think about the
current state of affairs. But when you ask them to
vision forward or to picture the future they want, it
puts them in a very different emotional state. It
actually shifts the energy in the conversation, in their
thinking and in their disposition.

This future orientation works in part because it gets
people out of trying to explain what hasn't worked in
the past and why things have "gotten so bad in the
first place". When people look at problems as they
exist today, few people want to volunteer to take
responsibility for the part they might have played in
how that problem emerged in the first place, but...the
future is a different story. The future hasn't happened
yet and is something that we can plan together and
where people feel like they have some agency (or
ability to influence what happens next), so they are
more optimistic about whatever it is that you need
them to do. The future focus shifts us out of a
conversation of trying to explain our failure (which
inspires no one) to planning our future (which

---

motivates action more effectively than talking about our current day crises or tough problems).

Future pacing is not just a technique in casemaking. Psychologists use this technique in their work when they want to motivate their clients. They'll say something like, "*close your eyes and think about where you'd like to be in one year...then in two years...then in five years...then in ten years. Imagine what it will feel like to reach your goals in one year...then your two-year goal... then your five-year goal...then the ten.*" Pacing people out into the future helps them to imagine living in a world in which the outcomes they've worked hard to achieve, actually come to fruition. It helps them to put their aspirations, hopes and dreams into a vision and subsequently, to see beyond the problems of today.

Health practitioners and motivational coaches also use this technique when they are trying to motivate their clients to overcome the barriers to health and wellbeing. Doctors, for example, might use it on a patient who is reluctant to take blood pressure medication because it sparks hair loss or some other negatively perceived appearance issue. The doctor would ask the patient about what they are looking forward to in the future — perhaps a daughter's wedding, a new grandchild on the way, retiring and buying a new house — whatever it is, the doctor would then say, "*well the only way you're going to be around for that future is to make sure that you take this medication with regularity. Don't miss out on the most important day in your daughter's life, or kissing your grand child for the first time, or enjoying your new life in retirement."*

The subtle art to future pacing is getting people to actually engage their intellect as well as their emotions. So, when they are imagining the future, ask them how they feel in that moment, what they see, what they smell, and to describe as much as they can about their vision. The more details they can offer, the more they own the vision as they see it (meaning the more they see themselves in it). Then ask them, who is helping them bring it to fruition – the community organizations, the businesses, the agencies, the friends and family. That helps them to envision the future as a collective one that involves the competencies and contributions of many.

Future pacing is an especially good technique when you need to deliver bad news. Bad news can be any news that you expect to have a negative impact on people's inspiration to do the work that you need them to do. For example, when you have to deliver bad news about the steady rise in homelessness or your organization's shrinking budget, or any number of other challenging issues. To make the case that people continue to stay the course (assuming that you've got good reason to think that is the wise course of action), pace them out a bit. Say something like, *"We are doing all we can to reduce homelessness in the region. We have a more aggressive set of policies and programs in place than ever before. But this challenge was not made in a day and it will not be solved in a day. It will take the steadfast resolution and commitment of this community over a number of years for us to make sure that every person in this region is safely housed, every night! With the investments that we are making to tackle this issue, by 2030 we expect to see homelessness finally be a problem of the past. Our goal is to make homelessness a brief, rare, and non-recurring experience for people. And with your continued and steadfast support, despite the bumps in the road we are seeing, we can do this!"*

The latter wouldn't be the only things that you might say but focusing the energy (and the data) on the future helps take the sting out of the early, unavoidable challenges of solving tough adaptive challenges.

A Message from the Future with Alexandria Ocasio-Cortez

One of the best recent examples of future pacing I've seen recently, comes from Representative Alexandria Ocasio-Cortez of New York in a video where she makes the case for the Green New Deal. In the video she asks, *"What if we actually pulled off a Green New Deal? What would the future look like? For the Green New Deal to become a reality we must be able to close our eyes and imagine it."*

The story format of the video takes advantage of the "slow brain" ideas identified in Strategic CaseMaking Principle #3. The video opens with her in the future talking about the existence of a bullet train, in a future time where we've already been able to achieve the Green New Deal.

We share selected passages from the video voiceover that Rep. Ocasio-Cortez providers. It is a clear example of this kind of future pacing.

Voiceover of Rep. Ocasio-Cortez:

Ah, the bullet train from New York to D.C. It always brings me back to when I first started making this commute. In 2019, I was a freshman in the most diverse Congress in history up to that point. It was a critical time. I'll never forget the children in our community. They were so inspired to see this new class of politicians who reflected them navigating the halls of power. It's often said, "You can't be what you can't see." And for the first time they saw themselves.

I think there was something similar with the Green New Deal. We knew that we needed to save the planet and that we had all the technology to do it. But people were scared. They said it was too big, too fast, not practical. I think that's because they just couldn't picture it yet. Anyways, I'm getting ahead of myself.

Let's start with how we got here…America became the biggest producer and consumer of oil in the world… We lost a generation of time we'll never get back, entire species will never get back, natural wonders gone forever. And in 2017 hurricane Maria destroyed the place where my family was from, Puerto Rico. It was like a climate bomb. It took as many American lives as 9/11. And in the next year when I was elected to Congress, the world's leading climate scientist declared another emergency. They told us that we had 12 years left to cut our emissions in half or hundreds of millions of people would be more likely to face food and water shortages, poverty, and death. Twelve years to change everything: How we got around, how we fed ourselves, how we made our stuff, how we lived and worked, everything.

The only way to do it was to transform our economy, which we already knew was broken since the vast majority of wealth was going to just a small handful of people and most folks were falling further and further behind. It was a true turning point. Lots of people gave up. They said we were doomed.

But some of us remembered that as a nation we'd been in peril before: the Great Depression, World War II. We knew from our history how to pull together to overcome impossible odds. And at the very least we owed it to our children to try.

The way it began was that Democrats took back the House in 2018 and then the Senate and the White House in 2020. Then we launched the decade of the Green New Deal, a flurry of legislation that kicked off our social and ecological transformation to save the planet. It was the kind of swing for the fence ambition we needed. Finally, we were entertaining solutions on the scale of the crises we faced without leaving anyone behind. That included Medicare for all, the most popular social program in American history.

We also introduce the federal jobs guarantee, a public option including dignified living wages for work. Funny enough the biggest problem in those early years was a labor shortage. We were building a national smart grid, retrofitting every building in America, putting trains like this one all across the country.

We needed more workers. That group of kids from my neighborhood were right in the middle of it all especially this one girl, Ileana. Her first job out of college was with AmeriCore Climate, restoring wetlands and bayous in coastal Louisiana. Most of her friends were in her union, including some oil workers in transition. They took apart old pipelines but got to work planting mangos at the same salary and benefits.
Of course, when it came to healing the land, we had huge gaps in our knowledge. Luckily, indigenous communities offered generational expertise to help guide the way.

...Those were years of massive change, and not all of it was good. When hurricane Sheldon hit southern Florida, parts of Miami went underwater for the last time. But as we battled the floods fires and droughts, we knew how lucky we were to have started acting when we did. And we didn't just change the infrastructure. We change how we did things. We became a society that was not only modern and wealthy, but dignified and humane too. By committing to universal rights like healthcare and meaningful work for all, we stopped being so scared of the future. We stopped being scared of each other. And we found our shared purpose.

...When I think back to my first term in Congress riding that old school Amtrack in 2019 all of this was still ahead of us and the first big step was just closing our eyes and imagining it.

We can be whatever we have the courage to see.

Principle #8:
Consequences of Inaction

In most communities, there is a long list of challenges that leaders are trying to solve. It is easy for our issues to get pushed aside for other more pressing and immediate "crises". In some cases, there may be other critical priorities that your stakeholders need to solve first. However, the case for our work is made much stronger when those stakeholders come to understand the urgency of the moment in the issues we raise too.

Unfortunately, our current practices usually put us in "crisis talk" mode. This means that we start to communicate about our issues from crisis-oriented language. Once upon a time, before the advocates on every major social issue used (and mis-used) the "language of crisis" to position their issue, that strategy might have worked. Today however, you will need to be a bit more creative and thoughtful in how you position the urgency of your issue, if you expect to elevate it on the long list of priorities for leaders.

Our task is to highlight what would happen if our stakeholders did nothing. If you are truly working on an important and compelling problem, it is likely that things would get much worse, if we kicked the can down the road. Powerfully communicate why immediate action gives us a better chance at solving the issue and call out the "adaptive leaders" who can see beyond the immediacy of today, toward the future we all deserve.

8. Consequences of Inaction

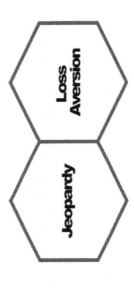

Reflection Questions:

🐾 Did I make it clear why there is urgency and a unique opportunity to solve this now?

🐾 Did I use data to paint a picture of the consequences of doing nothing about this issue as well as data to paint a picture of the positive consequences of immediate action?

🐾 Did I help my stakeholders get a strong sense of urgency about my issue?

Your Ticket to Implementing This Principle

This is one of the most important places in your case to leverage your data. Using data to paint a picture of the consequences of inaction gives this part of your case stronger legs. Start with the positive data – what happens 10, 15, 20 years from now if we lean in and invest our resources to resolve this issue…then present the alternative (vividly and with pictures), what happens if we let this moment pass without action? What happens if this moment passes with no action and we make no (or little) effort to change how we address this issue?

Sample Success Measures

☐ **KPI:** We are consistently using our data and narratives to bring a sense of urgency (not crisis) to our issues

☐ **Outcome:** Our stakeholders are no longer debating WHETHER we need to act, they are debating on how soon we need to act and what shape those immediate actions will take

☐ **Impact:** Our stakeholders begin prioritizing this issue for immediate action - on the agenda of their meetings, in the programs they offer, the investments they make, and services they make available

LOSS AVERSION &
THE PERCEPTION OF RISK

*"If we could be freed from our aversion to loss,
our whole outlook on risk would change."*
Alan Hirsch

Loss aversion is a cognitive bias that we all have, and it simply says that the pain of loss (or perceived loss) is stronger than the joy of any gain (or perceived gain) we have. If we could draw the basic philosophy on the back of a napkin, it would look like this:

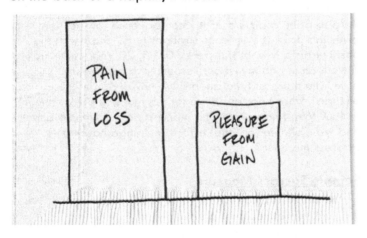

The idea was coined by legendary psychologists Amos Tversky and Daniel Kahneman out of their research in the early 90s and it is critical to understanding human decision-making. Fear of loss (or people's perception of loss) is a big part of what shapes their decision-making. This fear is so powerful that Chris Voss, one of the world's expert hostage negotiators often refers to loss aversion as "bending reality", because loss aversion distorts people's perception so much that it literally — bends their perception of reality!

Why are we so afraid of losing? Our aversion to loss is a strong emotion. The aversive response reflects the critical role of negative emotions (anxiety and fear) to losses. In other words, loss aversion is an expression of fear. This explains why we tend to focus on setbacks rather than progress — even when progress has been greater than any setbacks. Negative emotions, such as from receiving criticism, have a stronger impact than good ones, such as from receiving praise.

Simply put, we HATE to think that we are losing (or could lose anything). When we feel like our support for policies like affordable housing, health care reform, climate change or any other major system reform, will net us a loss of ANY kind, we reject the possible gains that might actually work in our favor (and in favor of those around us). This is true even when the gains we're likely to have far outweigh any loss we might suffer.

What's ironic is that on a lot of policy issues where people might actually experience gains (or improvements in their wellbeing or economic situation), they reject those policies for fear that somehow, they might have to give up, sacrifice, or lose something. And, as it turns out, most people are not very good at predicting what losses they would sustain or the magnitude of those perceived losses, in the first place.

So, the losses that people think they will sustain are rarely realistic or measured assessments of risk but typically represent their perceptions (magnified in abstract), which makes it almost impossible to get people to move forward when the perception of loss looms so large.

The takeaway for the changemakers among us, is this - if you want to move people forward and to have them respond to your call-to-action, you have to navigate this issue of loss aversion very strategically. You have to get the perception of loss back on the other side of the table. That is, get people to think about what they will lose if they fail to work with you to change those outdated systems for the better.

If your intent is to move them forward, you must find out how they feel they are losing because that's going to be the single dominating factor in their decision-making. Often, their perceptions are not even rational, but you have to understand those perceptions, in order to bend them. Feel of loss is what keeps people up at night. Nobody gets insomnia because life is good, instead they stay up worrying at night when they think they're losing something! They come to community or city council meetings, ready to shout down policymakers because they fear losing something – rarely because they have a "thank you" to offer. It's never rational and it's always bent based on their perception.

And here is the trick. You have to know what kinds of things they value so much that they are especially afraid to lose those things. Are they afraid to lose their health or the health of their loved ones? Is it fear that their children will not receive the advantages they need to do well in the economy that is coming? Is it fear that they will lose their economic security or their ability to retire with enough resources to be comfortable?

If you don't know what people are afraid to lose, you don't know what will motivate them to support your cause. So, find out! Ask them what they love about your community? What are they optimistic about in the future? What are they looking forward to in the next 10 years and what (if anything) makes them excited about those upcoming years?

When you start to get underneath these questions, you'll have what you need to pull them forward. Connect your issue to the things that they value most — the things they are most afraid to lose. And be clear about the ways in which, your call-to-action will help them avoid losing those things.

One caveat here should be noted: we never condone people holding onto bigoted or racist fears and our words should never enable them to do so. Sometimes people are holding onto things that are not conducive to the values of equity, fairness and inclusive communities. They may be holding onto bigoted practices, racialized policies that keep our communities divided or things like segregated neighborhoods, and they are afraid to lose those things. So, their perceptions of loss are connected to bigotry or racism or other outdated values.

If those are the things that people are afraid to lose, you need to do more digging. Usually if you get behind their bigoted or racist viewpoints, there lies a more basic fear. Fear that they won't belong to the new community practices that you are creating; fear that more equitable policies will leave them behind; fear that they will lose what little control they have over their own lives or worse, fear that they will lose the power to control other people's lives!

Once you've identified what's really underneath those viewpoints, you are in a much stronger position to unseat those views. In fact, you won't be able to unseat those views unless you can pinpoint the underlying fear.

Be clear from the outset, that you do not agree nor condone their bigoted or racist viewpoints. State that unequivocally and do not hedge on that (i.e. *I appreciate your concerns, but I do not support any policies that undermine people's dignity, worth, humanity or sense of belonging to this community*). Then connect their underlying fears back to the importance of the work you are trying to do (i.e. *So you are afraid this community will change and bring more people of color, well you should be more afraid that without exposure to a diversity of people, your children will be unprepared for the economy and the jobs that are coming. Those jobs will need people who can adapt easily to people of different races, faiths, background, sexual orientation and more. Those jobs will require that people have some fluency and effectiveness in engaging people authentically at every income or economic level. It is such a shame that your children may be unprepared for the jobs of the future and may be left behind unable to find a way to support your grandchildren, when so many others are using the diversity of their communities to prepare them for bright and prosperous futures. The jobs of the future are waiting for those children, but it looks like they will leave yours behind).*

Perhaps your example would be less direct than mine above and more tailored to the specific issue in your community or sector. But whatever it is, be clear that you'll need to explicitly put "loss" on the other side of the table. Be clear how people are losing out because they are delaying action on this issue and that those delays have costly consequences. When we do that, we are able to "bend their reality" back in our favor and put urgency back where it belongs.

We cannot change the fact that fear motivates action faster (and more profoundly) than their sense of benefits/gains. But we do have some control over how we help them balance out those fears — getting their perceptions of loss back where they belong. This is one of the most important casemaking techniques, so take the time to master it in your work.

TRY ME! No One Should Be Required to Demonstrate Odd-Defying Resilience to Live. We Need to Our Health Delivery Systems to Work Better

Can you imagine your community without its primary resources for wellness? Without the ability to deliver preventative and emergency care when you need it most? Well, if we fail to invest in improving our health delivery system, you won't have to imagine it. You may be forced to live it.

As the spread of the COV-19 virus has made painfully clear, our country needs to rethink how we deliver health care and prevent the spread of infectious diseases. Today as this deadly virus threatens to upend our entire way of life, there is new urgency in rethinking that system.

We have not built up an efficient system for handling health crises at the scale of what we are witnessing with COV-19 and public health experts warn that eventually, we will likely need to battle multiple health crises simultaneously. No one wants to be told that their hospital simply has no more beds or that their deceased loved ones have been stashed in a refrigerated truck outside because there is no more room for them in the hospital.

Every day that we fail to act affirmatively to prepare our health system for the worst-case scenarios, makes us more ill-prepared when those scenarios start to play out. Every day spent without the resources, investments and innovations necessary to improve our health delivery system, leaves us all in jeopardy.

When our healthcare professionals must spend their time wading through outdated practices, policies, equipment or institutional arrangements, to deliver care, nobody wins. We all lose.

As we rethink how health care is delivered and funded, it is unlikely that there will be any one person, one organization, one agency, or one company that will provide the complete solution, so our work has to be a collaborative effort. This work requires outstanding leadership and for us to be aware that what we're aiming to do is really, really hard on a ridiculously accelerated time scale.

We need to work as hard as we can collectively and as fast as we can. No one wants a repeat of the costly missteps during the early days of the spread of the COV-19 virus, so we have to focus. We must assess where our systems are strong, where they lack the necessary supports, and then, forge a new pathway that makes them even stronger. We have to use this moment to get serious about what it means to adapt our current health delivery system to the world that we have inherited. Not just to address the current COV-19 pandemic but for the next one already on its way.

Principle #9: Connect to the Value Proposition

For your audiences and stakeholders to WANT to work with you, they have to understand YOUR value proposition. They need to understand WHAT you are trying to do, how it will matter for them, and that you have the credibility or a proven track record to get results. Whether in business, sports or in social change efforts, people want to know that they are aligning themselves with "winners" and with people who can deliver on the promises they make. In a world where people are cynical about progress; where politicians promise the moon, stars and planets to get our votes but seldom deliver - the ability to deliver on those promises is what people value most.

Our task is to help our stakeholders and strategic partners see the value in working with us and to trust our expertise, approach, theory of change, adaptive leadership AND our record of success. This means that we must articulate our track record, our uniqueness in some way, and the value-add that a collaboration would offer up. This is our opportunity to share why our work, organization or coalition is best positioned to resolve the adaptive challenge or issue that we've identified in the case that we are making. This does NOT mean offering up a list of your collective accomplishments in resume fashion, it means helping people see your value in the way that YOU see your value.

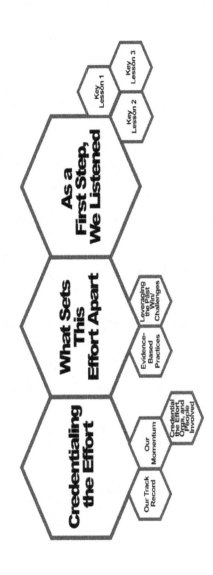

The Strategic CaseMaking™ Blueprint

9. Value Proposition

Reflection Questions:

🐾 Did I connect to the proven track record my organization or my coalition has on this issue? If we do not yet have a track record, have we established trust and credibility on this issue with our stakeholders and strategic partners?

🐾 Did I powerfully communicate the value of my organization or coalition with a strong, meaningful theory of change/action?

🐾 Did I share that theory of change/action with an explanatory metaphor to help give that theory real-time value to my stakeholders?

🐾 Did I use that theory of change/action and metaphor to also help my audiences and stakeholders understand THEIR role in working with my organization and/or our coalition?

Your Ticket to Implementing This Principle

Typically, people focus on the wrong information when they try to position their value proposition and make a plug for their work at the wrong place in the narrative - starting their messaging with who they are and what they do. Yikes! Instead, push that information down in the narrative AFTER you've established the urgency and relevance of the issues you are trying to solve. Then, use a strong theory of change/action to explain your work with an explanatory metaphor that can bring that theory to life! This is also a great place to bring in your impact data – data that shares what your impact has already been on this issue and to project with those data, what additional help/resources would do to advance your results even further. Don't assume here though "data" means only quantitative information, use qualitative data (stories, personal experiences, pictures, artistry, etc.) to share your value as well.

Sample Success Measures

- **KPI:** We are consistently sharing our theory of change/action with our stakeholders after they have bought into the urgency and relevance of this issue

- **Outcome:** Our stakeholders are operating with a clear understanding of our respective roles in resolving this issue

- **Impact:** Our stakeholders are consistently working with us in ways that align with our theory of change/action

HELPING YOUR STAKEHOLDERS AND STRATEGIC PARTNERS UNDERSTAND YOUR VALUE

Most of the time when people are offering advice about how to communicate a value proposition, they are talking about the solution you offer to your customers, clients or community. If you've followed the Strategic CaseMaking principles #1 thru #8 (all of the above) carefully, you are well on your way to doing that already. That is, all of the previous principles are pieces of the value proposition you are making about solving a particular set of adaptive challenges.

Principle #9 however is much more about the value that you (or your coalition, agency, organization, company, collective impact group, etc.) bring to the table. It would be a big mistake to assume that people inherently understand why you are important to the process of finding or implementing solutions simply because you have formed a coalition, or collective impact group or neighborhood association, etc. Your stakeholders and strategic partners need to trust you and understand your role as well.

Unless people understand the systems you are trying to change and why you are best to lead that work, they won't fully commit to your call-to-action. So, take the time to position YOUR work and YOUR role carefully. In other words, help your stakeholders and strategic partners understand the value you bring.

As you work to do that, here are some pro-tips and guidelines to help you. There are three fundamental steps with plenty of room for embellishment.

Step 1: Credential Your Leadership of the Effort.

- Share the track record (established history) of the team you've assembled.
  - o Do they have experience leading or collaborating on similar efforts (especially those that are community-driven, equity-focused or multi-sector)?
  - o Do they have experience addressing the specific issues on the table or are representing organizations that have this experience?

- Share how your effort builds on an important set of unique factors. It may be that the players around your table are unique or there is an unprecedented momentum emerging among stakeholders.

- Share what investments you and your collaborators have already made in addressing this issue and to what results.

- Share the ambitious vision that you have for solving that adaptive challenge collectively and why/how adding new strategic partners (i.e. new champions for this work) would help you gear up to do more.

- Share what core beliefs are driving this effort (*i.e. this effort exists because we believe there is great urgency and promise in providing support to community coalitions on the frontlines*).

Step 2: Share What Sets This Effort Apart from Past or Other Similar Efforts to Address This Issue.

- Share how the team assembled on this issue works together. Be specific. (*i.e. We do our work by identifying and testing new approaches in collaboration with other organizations, including both governmental agencies and private-sector entities*).
  - Are you working within a shared-equity model, advocacy or collective impact model?
  - How does each member or organization provide consistent and appropriate leadership to the effort?

- Share how the work is funded and how you have worked to leverage funding for your effort.

- Share how your team uses evidence-based and community driven practices to drive its work.

- Share how your working relationships, programs, policies, services or investments have shifted over time (ostensibly because of your growing knowledge of what works).

■ Share how you communicate your knowledge, best practices and other helpful supports back into the field or community in which you work.

■ Share how this group is agile and nimble in its ability to respond to the dynamism that adaptive challenges often evoke.

Step 3: As a First Step, We Listened.

■ Always describe your first steps as LISTENING! (i.e. *As a first step to working in this community, we listened and learned from our community partners - residents, agencies, organizations and companies*).
  o Drill down into specific lessons taken from this deep listening that serves as a guide to your work. Highlight any particular lessons related to: (1) overcoming challenges to cross-sector alignment and collaboration, (2) nurturing leadership from all parts of the community, professional field or country as a whole; (3) translating lessons from the community or field into broader practice; (4) engaging community authentically and respectfully; and (5) creating a culture of wellness and resiliency across the board.

- Share how your listening helped to nascent or emerging solutions on-the-ground or in practice. *(i.e. These efforts were under-powered because they were under-resourced and lacked the investments that could buy them the space and time to become stable anchors for resilience in their communities).*

- Share how the things you heard while in deep listening mode align (or differ from) existing practice or evidence. *(i.e. There has been important coalescence of the science on this issue that aligns with what we heard from community stakeholders).*

- Share the immediate next steps to be undertaken and why they require stakeholder alignment and new champions.

Building a Better Future, One Resilient Community at a Time

We believe the future of our planet will be shaped by how we invest our resources. The investments our cities make today, have a huge impact on the quality of our lives, our planet, and our opportunities for wellness in the short and long-term. Big infrastructure investments made in public transit systems, economic development and land development, to name just a few, are going to reshape the landscape of many cities across our nation.

For example, our cities are one of the biggest investors in smart city technology. In 2020 the investment made by cities in smart tech is expected to top $100 billion and grow to $135 billion by 2021. The critical decisions to invest and allocate these resources as well as the timing and scope of those investments, will ultimately determine who gets connected to opportunity and who is left out.

That's why we have organized a national network to support cities as they work to cultivate equitable and inclusive ways of deploying these needed resources. As a national network working to support and assist cities in making decisions that expand opportunity and equity for all, we know that our partnerships are what determine our success. Our network exists because of the commitment of leaders across this country who all believe that there is great urgency and promise in supporting the emergence of community-led, multi-sector networks to ensure that our cities make thoughtful decisions.

In this way, our network serves a unique role in influencing a "new normal" in how cities invest and advance the needs of their communities and residents. As a convener and a collective group of national thought leaders on the issues of community investment, public health, public policy, climate resilience, and the environment, we bring together expertise from philanthropy, business and local government to address cities' most urgent challenges.

Acting as a collective network, rather than as a single organization or government agency, we are able to respond more effectively to a wider range of adaptive challenges facing our cities. From COV-19, to affordable housing, to education, opioid addiction, infrastructure needs and disaster planning, our network makes it possible for cities to get the best advice, counsel and relevant partners to the table quickly. With this network structure, we can respond nimbly and directly to the urgency of the challenges our cities face.

We know that our cities (large and small, urban and rural) are ground-zero for a range of adaptive challenges that can only be solved through multi-sector efforts alongside the voices, involvement and lived experience of community residents. That's why our network was created and why our nation has a huge stake in its success.

Principle #10: Results Framework Tracking Meaningful Metrics of Success

Like it or not, we live in a brand-new world of data. Data is collected everywhere and in every aspect of our lives. Many of us have become fairly sophisticated in the collection of data about our issues and our stakeholders have come to expect that we have data to back up our claims that our approaches and solutions are working. The good news is that usually, the data is on our side. The impacts of the work that many of us are doing to improve our communities, cities and regions can be shown through an intentional focus on collecting the appropriate data.

Yet, in order to make a compelling case for more support, we need to wield this data carefully and strategically. Having a results framework makes it clear to stakeholders what the goal posts are and how they can trust that we're serious about driving toward the outcomes we laid out in our case. This means that we need to take seriously the charge of getting our numbers right. Understanding what the return-on-investment (ROI) is of our programs, policies and investments is critical — especially in today's world where so much of this information is easily calculated. In addition, we need to ensure that we are also calculating the social-return-on-investment (SROI) or the impacts of our programs, policies and investments for our community. Seeing both the ROI and SROI next to each other, helps us provide empirical evidence.

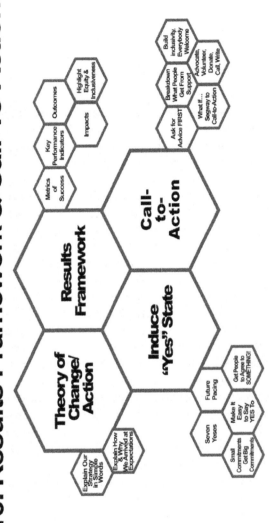

10. Results Framework & Call-To-Action

Reflection Questions:

🐌 Did I share the results framework (assessment of the short-term, mid-term & long-term outcomes as measures of success)?

🐌 Did I share my theory of change/action to help my stakeholders understand what makes me confident that we will generate the outcomes outlined in our case?

🐌 Did I explain the process and frequency in which we'll review outcome metrics against our stated goals?

🐌 Am I calculating and sharing as part of my impact assessment, the ROI and SROI of my work?

Your Ticket to Implementing This Principle

Of all the data that you can share, perhaps the most powerful is the social return on investment (SROI). The SROI usually calculates the monetary value of your impact. So, we invested in after school programs for youth but the value of what we got back was much broader than youth performing at grade level. We may have also provided a safe place for youth to be after school, keeping them off the street and out of trouble and it may have resulted in better job prospects or earnings for those youth. Our ability to calculate the value of those outcomes matters!

Sample Success Measures

☐ **KPI:** We have defined a meaningful set of metrics, that we are consistently collecting and sharing broadly/transparently as part of our casemaking.

☐ **Outcome:** Our stakeholders have a clear understanding of what success means to us – in both qualitative and quantitative terms.

☐ **Impact:** Our stakeholders are more committed to our work because they understand that we are results focused and they help us to gather up the data we need to demonstrate progress on our issues.

INDUCING A "YES" STATE:
SPOILER ALERT, METRICS MATTER

There has always been a large body of scholarly research on the art or psychology of persuasion (some call it, the science of influence). In whatever variety it comes, the focus has always been – how do we get people to follow our lead and say "yes" to our call-to-action. For changemakers working to improve your communities, there is both an art and science involved in how we make our case.

First, let's just acknowledge that many companies and individuals use methods—consciously or not—that behavioral science has shown are effective in getting people to say "yes", whether in making a sale, gaining cooperation or consensus, or coaxing charitable donations. When life insurance companies offer—with "no obligation"—a flashlight and keychain to AARP (American Association of Retired Persons) members who agree to let the company send them information, they are using an empirically-based persuasion principle. And there are many such practices that make it easier for us to persuade people to lean in just long enough to give ourselves the opportunity to share how our work to bring about equitable system change, might benefit all of us and the communities that surround us.

One of the most compelling is the work you can do to induce a "yes" state. If you've ever been on a sales room floor for any appliance or to buy a car, you've been exposed to this principle. The car salesman might casually talk to you but ask a series of questions of you, as you browse the showroom floor. Some of those questions are meant to clarify if you are a serious buyer or just a "looky loo" perusing the salesroom floor as spectator rather than a buyer. Once they've established that, they'll ask a series of questions meant to induce a "yes" state: the more often they can get you to say yes, even to small questions, the more likely they'll be able to get you to say yes to the big purchase.

So, the salesperson might start by saying something like, *"If I could get you the best financing rate on this car today, would you consider buying it today?"* Once you've said yes, they'll proceed with more small talk and then say something like, *"and if I could get the make, model and color of your choice right here in the showroom today, would you consider buying it today?"* Then, rinse, wash, and repeat...something like, *"And if I could get you a price that could beat anybody in this area, even under MSRP, then would you sit down with me and consider buying today?"* And so on...

The salesperson's purpose of those questions both qualifies you as a serious buyer and induces a yes state. The salesperson is aiming at getting you to say "yes" at least seven times — why? The rule of seven in marketing is clear — the chances of the person saying "yes" to the big ask after seven yeses, increases dramatically. So, they want to throw you a pitch (or ask you softball "yes" questions) so that on the 7th throw, you are softened up and ready to go!

So, my friends, I'm not asking you to become a car salesman or peddle a marketing slide deck around with you. But I am asking you to be present to the idea that there are subtle ways of helping people connect with your call-to-action that are about human psychology. The more we understand those techniques, it allows us to be at least as persuasive as corporate marketers who peddle products to us (most of which we don't need and are over-priced).

So, get in the habit of preparing questions when you pitch your ideas that get people in the habit of saying yes. Something like,

- *"If I could show you how to improve health outcomes for the people in this community by at least 24% over the next year, with an investment the size of your paper towel budget, would you consider hearing me out?"*

- Or like this, *"If I could show you how to bring new resources to this community to improve the health and wellbeing of children in this community, with little to no personal investment, would you hear me out?"*

- Or, *"What if I could show you how to revitalize this community — bringing new playgrounds, open green space, bike zones, and more off-street parking, would you want to hear more about that?*

The questions you raise should be "no brainers". They should be easy "yes" questions that you know your stakeholders and strategic partners can say yes to. Be mindful as well that the questions should accurately reflect what your call-to-action would actually do! Do NOT misrepresent what you can offer but give people a sense of what the benefits would be of leaning into your call-to-action.

To make this technique even more effective, make the "yes" question coincide with one or more of the success metrics you've laid out in your results framework. Like this,

- *"What if I could show we can bring down infant mortality rates in this community by 20% in 5 years, would you be interested?"*

- Or something like this, *"What if I told you that we have raised $13 million dollars to support pilot programs and system innovations that are going to reduce homelessness in this community by more than 25% over the next 5 years, is that of interest to you?"*

- Or this one, *"Some people in this community are concerned about the number of children who have anxiety, depression or considering suicide. What if there are some pretty simple ways that all of us can help cut that number in half in just under a year? It's been done in other communities, why not in ours?"*

People genuinely want to nod yes to those questions. Contrary to popular belief, they genuinely want to hear good news and when they hear more about the  metrics of success that you've outlined for your work, you genuinely have a better shot at getting them to say "yes" to your call-to-action.

So, ASK QUESTIONS! Practice developing some good ones — ones that get people to think about the possibilities of your success and that help them understand your metrics for measurement. The opportunity to pull your audience forward using this technique is made even more effective when you pair it with your metrics of success.

When you use this pro-tip, you are able to pull people into a conversation saying "yes" before you get to the big ask and then, you can inspire them to share the good news of what your organization, agency or collaborative team is working on. It is also important to say again that metrics matter -no matter what — to our casemaking. They help convince our stakeholders and strategic partners that we are serious, that we have identified very specific outcomes and that we're willing to be held accountable for those outcomes.

Here's Our Results Framework. Track Our Progress, Help Us Celebrate the "Wins" and Improve in Areas Where We Are Struggling

From the beginning of this effort, we have been relentlessly results-focused and accountability driven. We shared our results framework (the metrics we would use to ensure we were on target) early on in our process and we invite you now to help us evaluate how we're doing.

We've done quite a lot this year. So far, we've made significant and measureable progress in reducing our housing shortage and making homes a priority.

✓ We completed a strategic audit and action plan for our work this year.
✓ We developed and ratified Memoranda of Understanding (MOUs) among our collaborating organizations.
✓ We elevated leadership commitment on this issue with more than a dozen large employers in the region now championing this issue and committing resources.
✓ We have created stronger visibility on this issue so that media coverage, social media and local conferences all reflect a focus on this issue.
✓ We have strengthened the capacity of our advocacy partners by raising more than $25 million to support innovative programs for

communities in the region.

✓ We have reduced point-in-time counts of people experiencing homelessnes in our region through stronger lease-up rates.

✓ We have increased the ability of service providers to ramp up the operations, scale, and quality of services they offer.

✓ We have worked in strong cross-sector partnerships (with the consolidated school district, our teachers union and the largest hospitals across the region).

We are winning in the work to change the trajectory of this issue across our region. But there is stil much work to be done. We need public, nonprofit, and private sector leaders to join forces and meet this challenge head-on and with renewed vigor.

For the next three years of our partnership, we expect even bigger, measurable results that will shape our pathway to the broader impacts we are working toward. While some of the details around the next phase of our work will evolve over time, we believe it is important to chart out the pathway as we see it today. By 2028, we will:

• make homelessness rare, brief and non-recurring by accelerating our strategy and working with a wider range of partners

• eliminate chronic homelessness across our region

• have created an even stronger safety net for people who are housing insecure and vulnerable in the context of our housing system

- we will triple our capital raise on this issue – bringing in more than $150 million to support our strategies on this issue
- we will close the racial gap as it relates to homeownerrship and affordable rental housing, to ensure that people of color in our region are benefitting as much as other groups from our success
- we will strengthen the capacity of the community stakeholders and partners to scale the programs, services, and/organizational practices that deepen their impact by investing in new ideas and innovative solutions
- we will identify and build public support for a permanent revenue stream to ensure we are never again struggling to support the housing needs of so many people in our region

Join us to help transform our response to the housing needs of this region. Help us champion this effort in your network. You can help generate the groundswell of support we need to ensure the health of our region.

"We are unstoppable.

Another world is possible"

Practice, Practice, Practice Starts Here

Like any other practice, Strategic CaseMaking™ takes practice. Take this opportunity, having reviewed the principles to elevate your casemaking by using the pages that follow to practice. What would a strong We/Why statement look like? What dominant narratives are you reframing to avoid the backfires that often plague our attempts to engage new champions to our work?

Take one or more of your externally-facing materials (your campaign materials, regional plan or strategic plan, your website or mission statement) and use the examples provided in the last sections of this Guide to practice. Think about how your stakeholders and strategic partners will receive what you're saying and what elements of your casemaking might best help to pull them forward.

Backfires, Backpack and Bedtime Stories

- **What are the Backfires We Get as We Try to Make the Case on This Issue?**
  _____
  _____
  _____
  _____

- **What are the Backpacks We Get as We Try to Make the Case on This Issue?** _____
  _____
  _____
  _____

- **What are the Bedtime Stories That People Tell Us When We Try to Make the Case on This Issue?**
  _____
  _____
  _____
  _____
  _____
  _____
  _____
  _____

Frame the Adaptive Challenge

The world is changing rapidly. How will our call-to-action on this issue prepare us for the world that is coming, the economy that is coming, the demographic & technological shifts that are coming, and for the planet we will inherit?

- Our adaptive challenge is: _____
  _____
  _____
  _____
  _____

- This adaptive challenge matters to all of us because: _____
  _____
  _____
  _____

- These are the resources, institutions, practices and skills sets we will need to solve this adaptive challenge:_____
  _____
  _____
  _____
  _____
  _____
  _____
  _____

Systems Change, Equity & Inclusion

To solve the adaptive challenge we face, we must be clear about the systems that need rethinking and how we can embody an inclusive process as we redesign those systems and achieve equitable outcomes as the result.

- What systems would need to change for us to solve this adaptive challenge? _____
  _____
  _____
  _____
  _____

- What are the levers that drive change in those systems? _____
  _____
  _____
  _____

- What will equity and inclusion look like in the context of our call-to-action on systems change?
  _____
  _____
  _____
  _____
  _____
  _____

The Bridge of Understanding

Let's be clear about who our champions are, as well as who could be new champions of our work, once we get them on the bridge of understanding.

- Who are the people, agencies, institutions, organizations, corporations, houses of worship, community residents, and others, who can influence change of those systems? _____
  _____
  _____
  _____
  _____

- What do we need from these potential champions? What's our theory of change about what happens once they are on the bridge of understanding? _____
  _____
  _____
  _____

- What are they afraid to lose? And, what are their dominant narratives about this issue?
  _____
  _____
  _____

Principles of Strategic CaseMaking™ #1 through #5

Our "WE"/ "Why" is _____

_____

_____

_____

The dominant narratives and negative disruptors we need to navigate around are _____

_____

_____

Our "Story of Us" begins with _____

_____

_____

_____

_____

We will use data to anchor our case in these ways _____

_____

_____

_____

We will use these metaphors to make the systems visible that need to be changed and to highlight the equity issues we are trying to tackle _____

_____

_____

Principles of Strategic CaseMaking™ #6 through #10

OUR responsibility to solve this issue is:
_____
_____
_____

The trends on the strategic horizon that will help us position this issue are_____
_____
_____

If we take no action to solve this, what are the likely consequences (in the short and long term_____
_____
_____
_____

We are best positioned to solve this because_____
_____
_____
_____

We will use the following success metrics to remain accountable to our stakeholders: _____
_____
_____
_____

Notes and Reflections

Notes and Reflections

Notes and Reflections

Notes and Reflections

Notes and Reflections

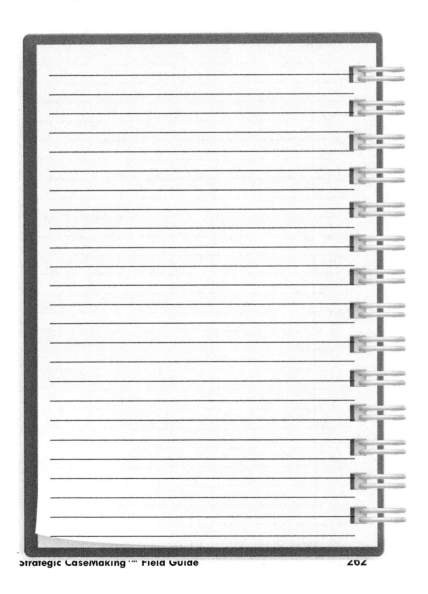

Notes and Reflections

Notes and Reflections

Notes and Reflections

About TheCaseMade

Our mission is to transform communities all over the world by helping leaders build the public will to intentionally tackle the issues of equity and inclusion. We work across sectors and issue areas to help leaders understand the power of Strategic CaseMaking™ and to use it as a critical instrument for systems change. Our approach is to use trainings, workshops, community engagement and consulting to deliver resources that are transformative.

At TheCaseMade we help leaders make the case for systems change by aligning stakeholders and organizing their resources in a deliberate system change strategy. We work across sectors and issue areas to help leaders understand the power of effective Strategic CaseMaking™ and to use it as a critical instrument for system change. Let us:

- facilitate a training or workshop to engage your staff, board, community partners and residents in Strategic CaseMaking™
- conduct a review of your public-facing materials to help provide recommendations for stronger CaseMaking™
- support your executive team as strategic advisors in public-facing campaigns, strategic initiatives and cross-sector collaboration
- help refine your system change strategy by incorporating a meaningful way to measure success (a results framework)

About the Author

Dr. Tiffany Manuel (DrT) is the President and CEO of **TheCaseMade**, works with hundreds of passionate social change leaders, changemakers and innovators around the United States to help them powerfully and intentionally make the case for systems change. By aligning their community stakeholders around the kind of deep systems changes that can improve population outcomes, these leaders are able to grow their impact, scale their programs, and harness the investments they need to improve their communities.

Trained as a social scientist, DrT is committed to building the capacity of changemakers and leaders to grow their social impact. DrT has worked to expand opportunity for low-income workers, families and communities through 25+ years of professional and

volunteer experience spanning the private and non-profit sectors, government and academia. DrT is passionate about translating the insights harvested from this work to increase opportunities for public deliberation and public will-building. DrT holds doctorate and master's degrees in public policy from the University of Massachusetts Boston, a master's degree in political science from Purdue University and a bachelor's degree in political science from the University of Chicago.

Made in the USA
Monee, IL
17 June 2021